I, CAUSTIC

MOHAMMED KHAÏR-EDDINE
translated by **JAKE SYERSAK**
with a postface by **KHALID LYAMLAHY**

ISBN: 978–1–933959–53–5

Cover images and artwork by Moa Bennani
Untitled, 2019, oil on canvas, dyptych, 200 x 100 cm

Design and typesetting by Mark Addison Smith

Litmus Press is a program of Ether Sea Projects, Inc., a 501(c)(3) non-profit literature and arts organization.

Litmus Press publications are made possible by the New York State Council on the Arts with support from Governor Kathy Hochul and the New York State Legislature. This project is also supported in part by an award from the National Endowment for the Arts. Additional support for Litmus Press comes from the Leslie Scalapino–O Books Fund, The Post-Apollo Press, and individual members and donors. All contributions are fully tax-deductible.

LITMUS PRESS
925 Bergen Street #405
Brooklyn, New York 11238
litmuspress.org

SMALL PRESS DISTRIBUTION
1341 Seventh Street
Berkeley, California 94710
spdbooks.org

Cataloging-in-publication data is available from the Library of Congress.

I, CAUSTIC

MOHAMMED KHAÏR-EDDINE
translated by **JAKE SYERSAK**

I, CAUSTIC 9

Postface: The "Plural Atom" of Khaïr-Eddine's Words
Khalid Lyamlahy 155

A Note on Translation
Jake Syersak 165

Hey whoa auntie heyo there little miss strangulationista on the cross shooting glances back and forth between I and the eye of a causticity-laced mongrel-faced father made so by an unsusceptible insect! We're going to town overturning tables just as easily as any man Gal-pal-o'-mine O Fuck You in Your Face Right here and now in this restaurant where I'm slapping on a pair of culottes and spectacles to boot to get a better load of my portrayal of lousy over-the-top-ness. Limping wasn't an option. Seeing through the luminosity was… The city's inter-intesti-gurgling. Sneers and tears slip their little nothingness in more and more crocodylinaeatory along the rim of a coffee cup's promising whoever stumbles across it a whole new way of seeing how teething works or plainly put the repeal of certain lawful rights at the behest of His Adroit Majesty Who awaits us patiently in the stables where our counterfeit currency takes aim against the agrarians' gold virtually showing off by now And what's it to you? Talking to… Mocking who? Really shaking him down. Getting down and dirty. Downright sick. Boring the shit out of the other. I've killed him Don't you all realize what that little So-and-so wanted to do? Make me look like a fool no more no less. So yes I wrapped my hands around his throat. The real work got done under-ground-elsewhere Not here Under the overwhelmingly complicit shadow of soiled ritualistic rags passing us by But I haven't forgotten I owe you my situation: What a nice little runabout this was.

Lift me up, Causticity. Crown my skull, Ink. I guzzle your quills. Surround the Madonna. Pffft-scape! The glory of the father the untraceable gibberish-spitting father. His speeches drove a nail straight through my reign's putrefaction. My move, Cyclops! Everyone into the chamber. No no no, let's regroup, inside the surgical bloc, inside the operating room, inside the theater. Inside the other trance Oh what succulence! Put your faith in my armaments and patrolwomen. Don't write them off: Heed my words get the hell out of my sight Those goddamned termites swarming the exposed beams without unscrewing my perspective first without a second thought to my immanence however jovial Jubilant rose-colored upon the never-ending whiteness It's not even the rainy season Not one seedling of corn! Not one diplomatic accord! Not one foreign exchange! Not one person willing to hold their feet to the flames! Lyreless men you are forgiven! Enough of your ideas already Take my gold my shadow my harems and just leave me the hell alone already! Now I am become the king transformed into a socialist. Enough already, enough!

He strikes a deal with the devil But one who won't be in our corner anymore For the year petered out between bouts of collective work and blood-soaked rumors. Everyone over at my place But I wasn't feeling alone enough I riveted them to my putrefied flesh. I'm here feeding some sorta guy who's absolutely oblivious to it spits fistulas at the good heavenly blood greening over faster than it can run itself off. I watch myself disintegrate into gluttony and an utter vastness of laughter, very tastefully, too. Wrangle them into line using only my mind. I stand my ground, refusing to listen; he loses it, knowing they've been gobbled down—his caiman eggs. The Causticity toys with his entrails from the inside out. I issue a national death certificate and force his headquarters to split wide open. Prone to imagining himself dead spread out stiff as a board sucking dry the lands that never forgave him. Skin aflame under his epidermis. It was, or so it seemed, a form of laughter by other means. He was tearing us limb-from-limb with his internalized death. Not a word of it got out, not one. Maybe he was coming around to versifying our heads from the dead coming around to baptize them Axe, Termite-mound, Nail. Waiting until his casket was slung over our shoulders to watch us sweat. Yeh, shit himself. Again, that earthly dilettante! Devoured me for nothing. Eye on the asthma, rising, rising. Indulging themselves in the rottenest of copulations. Disemboweled the spans of time a tree's nothingness grows of, is composed of. Thundered in the bile-like gold heretofore calling rat every last squirming under the bar counter's filthy lack of leg space. The tumbler drowned down its water. Through the limit of being my night funneled its lukewarmness. Yet nothing seemed very festive. The streetlights (there were none) would've given the blood of God to look me up and down. The day after, I made my way into the cemetery to see if I was still there. I was neither under the entryway's slab nor under the trees which were listening in on me, disseminating my every move. The birds had ceased to admonish the earth and its grassy plots. Everything was going back to normal. Things inveighed from the inside. He'd composed his book without telling me, but I was sure that every second that went by outside of it meant a life that wouldn't run smoothly. There was no future for this man. The world of highways, as varied as it was, put up with too much to permit him anything outside of a shouting match. Nevertheless, it reeled inward, ignited a quarrel, striking just the right nerves to invent a comely death. A real toad, half owl-ing, half cooing. And that toad over there, how could it croak? We treat language, the word, as if it were some quotidian meal. Everything's encrypted, including my head. And so he'd pulled it off after all these years. Stayed behind to pierce the stalks' ears. His country was the voyage. His home? Nonexistent. People here and there and everywhere claimed that he'd slain the gods and carved out his mother's glottis. In honor of his decline, ten new mosques were raised to fill the void his stature left behind; nevertheless, he'd unleashed a pack of hyenas all with the loveliest fangs there were to gnaw away at the sacred stone slowly but surely. It was said that no ancestors whatsoever would be permitted.

Midnight. The alcoholic no one needs. She motioned to have the bones scraped and belly filled of one who would pass the vast majority of his time in a pool of urine watching television and maybe picking his nose damning a heavenly expanse to hell I wasn't aware of despite providing it with a foundation via my spasmodic colic. She had imagined him as one capable of conspiring to build a paradise of his own ruins. A simple home with meadows made for stripping away your ear or eye while you slept. But he would freeze up as soon as she made a noise. Africa smoldered inside his loins and his blood was forced from his heart.

A rolling boil of feverish fermentations. Not one scream save the thunder or Hiroshima that fucked up glory. Not one single star that digs its horns into you and modifies the lines of your palmistry. No, not even a man! He'd never even been. Maybe it was desirable to view him as someone whose only request, ever, was to have someone else make sure he was glutted. He'd have been incapable of doing this himself. It was an unutterable body dispossessing itself without stopping. A permanent torture or else a scrivener. A gravelly-bird-man whose movements atrophied anything and everything that might've reassembled itself into the slightest semblance of a human being. He'd studied the notion of crime. Crime, for him, was nothing less than script. Script that had no use for the alphabet. He was no longer conducting a form of guerrilla warfare but a cyclone of go-sand-blast-God-get-your-feet-in-the-glue. Having written it down, it became a tornado babbling towards you:

She'll start singing her song just to displease me,
That gassy little girl! A veritable statue
the anthropophagus was tasked with decrypting.
I'm dedicating this to all those who aren't able to,
to those who can't stand being lumped together as one single entity.
And hey why not even to tomorrow that grandiose dump
no one's going in or out of.
This gentleman's laughter has descended into forgetfulness.
Comrades, who among you wages war! Any of you guilty?

But while he sought out order neither cement nor the clay of beaten earth stood ready to consecrate, his arms were whittled into shrivels, until he was forced to devour himself. Dwindling down to nothing more than skin and bones, He'd written it out, stupefied, this Mister Refuse-useful-to-our cause; sooner or later we'll have to lay him out; sooner or later we'll be lounging over his debris of night-hound-serpentine-time-keeping-scar-which-keeps-on-bleating! The minute a man does like us and can't muster the means necessary to switch bodies, he's an anarchist, you say! You sprain your brains responding to what isn't made from your matter. Either you'll be corralled by the street-sweepers or the police. They'll suck those toxins out one way or another, whether you like it or not. His burning corporeality was colliding with road signs, the night of sperm and sweat and fireflies rouging-up everything but the telephone poles. His earthen breast of boiled juices sowing his voice and his inaudible snoring. She on no beach I was familiar with, over a bed of tobacco leaves Without a doubt we'd grown mold there, together, we two—using some glue I've no clue what. This body dangling by its rhombi, feet swaying at the end of a rope guzzling the lice of the crossed-out nomad tenebrous after ejaculation the lion eyes extinguishing their flames in the earth their teeth broken up into thirty bridles and some centuries of royalty that perpetually refused to play by another's rules Twelve thousand prisoners for whom the plasma burns That one voluntarily identifies with the rebels another title it distinguishes Some palaces are accounted for via the banks in order to avoid the ruin of the family plot And his corpse what of his corpse There's no record of any. Keep writing: His yielding corpse yielded the architectural epicenter wrenched open the throat of the parricidal terrain And his sonorous corpse inside my corpse responded to every ambush The king was finishing up his maggoty sponge bath was feeding the bleaks fish hooks were rare a king isn't enamored as easily with other industries as he is with those manufacturing arms imported from Italy Let's not talk about that asshole! He who is undeserving of being referred to by a sentiment as overtly existent as that He knows what he's about He sows an excess of emotion throughout the carpet so you won't get all closed off all the while eyeing anyone bearing gifts with an air of suspicion simultaneously Someone anyone close in on him Sabotaging the slightest pebble sucking the fraternal sperm straight from the cock of well-established writers straight from the credibility of the incredible all while resembling the wormy belt of a devil who hastens through everything sapping a tree to its end May he enlighten himself! Go nowhere but into the still absent silence LET'S CUT HIM DOWN! He wasn't looking for a bullseye He was wary not only of us but other wrecks too that viciousness and rage would churn out an unpredictable tornado You asses, listen to me, I weep the faith of bloodlines-rearing-up-large-as-my-scepter Tremendous absolutely tremendous This endeavor forges ahead If you go inside you're never coming out Caustically he writes wanders commands reels ever outward comes apart without ever completely catastrophizing Hear-ye! Pour a little beer into that inkwell of his. Polish the shoes his nothingness is. Quicken your death. What I want is to remain alone my birds copulating on the rocks finally vaulted shut You're from where Just give the word, we'll re-arm! May verse or stony machine be faulted. Only the freshest of breasts circulate my palette, wrenched from the tree of science. I've purchased women and directors without talent. Talent has gone into exile. Africa as a whole can't stand it. No one will ever catch up with Mr. Talent. He worries only the guinea pigs running tests on themselves by themselves but we all concede that a population bloated with talent doesn't bode well for those in power I'm indifferent to talent but don't take that to mean I'm preoccupied with it Don't take that to mean it inconveniences me invalidates me kinglettes me I'm really rather exhausted May they simply forbid all talent here It wouldn't know how to grow in this clarity of ours in this *no-man's-land* of our beautifully-situated sunlight oft-quoted in brochures and abodes of our real estate agents And anyways the fact of the matter is it's our countryside and its leathery phlegm there's also our desert nights which bestow him a place of honor over our heads Talent will only bite the dust boorishly under our sun Allow Talent to be born and to evolve out in the cold and let's consider our sun as a land off-limits.

Insignificant scriveners of the palace rhododendron ivy your eruptions from the mantises' bellies are overrunning me erupting from me with laughter those other underlings of yours O.S.2 and P.3 loaned out long ago to my same old enemies there's a somewhat pretty flower ripe for the plucking let's drop it into a vase of milk into this furnace In all likelihood that's exactly what's going to bring us together Repeal any act of law decreeing talent's got the freedom to exist What an infinitely bourgeois term talent is Go get up in talent's face and tell it what an abscessed little hellion it is Grotesque or violent talent who gives a shit don't give them an inch!

He who is tattooed no longer matters to us. Only compost. Sprawling outward with neither constraint nor root. The sort of guy who'd die on his way up his publisher's stairs. With neither woman nor just cause behind his eyes darting here and there and just as often sawing right on through. Straight into another Atlas-worthy attempt at language. Tearing through the slings and arrows but grinning and enveloping the gist with darkness. He is wasting away, he who is tattooed. He's slaughtered those who so much as sought entry into his voluminous crate of incendiary wicks. The only order they'd ever established was a script with its lines burnt out from the very start, the only communal sense an association of age-old scorpions for the insects to peruse Nevertheless he himself is going to waste, slowly but surely, underneath his ledger. A wormy verse had already ascended the public prosecutor's office, crawling up the walls of the auditorium, where the photo of its spitting-image was rooting out its deserted obsolescence.

here is his text:

black on grey alucite fungus moth the grammatical fist Am I not communicable My father did little else but augment you inside his halos and his grease Your leopard's latching onto my toe lickety split But I'll endeavor to step aside It's bound to release such a burst of sunlight neither bomb nor telegraphy will omit constraining the array I rattle out my teeth with. After a few drinks he would venture some harsh words and commit petty crimes. It quickly became clear who'd maim who for a glass of vodka! No shame. His typewriter did the work while he slept. A thousand ants hauled out his nodule. He hollowed out time in a single gesture. No longer daydreamed of screaming sands where several lumberjills once seated a male specimen after stripping him down to nothing—there were no clothes aside from a sack of hemp carefully sewn together and then burned here and there by the ends of cigars. Back then politics were going swimmingly. Draping a protective caparison around all those who'd opened fire on a standing guard or emaciated dog. Politics reeked of its very spermatozoa. The Moroccan Goumiers and Senegalese were strewn about the sidewalks, holding their arms out to the passersby, as if to signify that their death wasn't exactly the same! But every time it was a trap, an ineffable lesson carried out by the army whose duty it was to surround the city in ever broader strokes. The cesspools, too, reeked of a god's passion, one who stood accused of high treason. Every ten minutes he would release another wingèd shark. These monsters rewarded me with revolver or rifle bullets whenever I wandered about in search of the paradise they'd assured me at my school desk I'd find somewhere out there. After each lesson, the instructor would trace the sovereign's head out on the board. This was his usual style of instruction, but all he managed to do was solidify a pitiful myth in our immemorial blood, which he knew deep down in his heart, sooner or later, would be jettisoned. Near the school, a conspirator had been shot. The noise of the gunfire seemed indistinguishable from applause to me. Only later did I come to understand it was about the liberation of an entire world and not a single people rolled up into its secular complexes—wrists tied, twisted, more and more strenuously bewildered, and baring its backside to police batons, woven chicote whips, switches, and other means of persuasion! There was no room left in this eye of mine which, as though thrown into a vat of sulfuric acid, had melted away like a body without its bones. Love, up to that point, had remained unknown to me! Nevertheless, I was compelled to seek a new skeleton for so extravagant a people. I devoted myself to the research of a science that would be capable of creating not just one but millions of them. I thought I would proceed by rending the flaccid body open, stripping out its entrails, strewing previously consumed bits of barley around me for the birds to pick over... But the body seemed to me as void as the skeleton. The stray cats around my neighborhood must have made short work of it! The people probably fled. The body of the people would be found later on in the grassy steppe, healing with a will all its own. Its ancestors had put blood to the test. This body cried out in no unclear terms that the strength they'd bequeathed it wasn't even enough to defend against the common jackal, much less any turncoat of a king. And so it was: a people sent packing! This land hadn't belonged to them prior to or even after the Crusades, Crusades which they'd assured us were worthwhile, in terms of providence. The tribal leaders preferred exile, the coal mines, and the cold air to a lifetime's submission to the sovereign and his police squad. They refused to pay taxes, to fatten the fakirs, or participate in any other tragedies that were handed down from Islam. They knew that this religion, rolled out for them upon rotted-out banquet tables, arose from a place of passive aggression and that it would collapse into nothing less than organized—arbitrary—slavery. The people examined, studiously, those values and false claims that had so meticulously made their way under its skin. Making itself a promise to compose a theatrical production eluding any metrical or temporal law, opening eyes to those corpses swallowed by history, passed over in silence, and whose names and loyalties someone had underhandedly modified to be used to their advantage. The entire thing would have to restructure its atomic nature from the names and addresses stowed underground by the tyrants of the world, eaten away by or short-circuited through the eyes of an omniabsent god whose weight, nevertheless, bore down upon his back and the inside of his lungs. Only the ruins of the latest dynasty had been kept in pristine condition. Every king's death had left, in its wake, a cyclops, one who would tear down his palaces and his whorehouses and just as quickly swap them out for no less obscene complexes. Royalty wandered its aimless way throughout the territory, down the ages, hoisting its laughter as high as the sky and boasting a self-proclaimed power that'd been bestowed upon them by a well-meaning but no less corpse-like god. The existing orders were no more, unable to hang on. Work stopped on a dime. The creature had to be worshipped and its legs bent back behind its head to get a good look at what it had become. Let the ingrates and the unbelievers say what they will. This was a worthwhile task. The king's speech was crystal clear on this point. They always ended it with Long-Live-Us-the-Immensity. The fquih and the adjoining crocodiles donning djellabas would end their sermons before even delivering them. The lesser people of the market embittered by the ever-increasing taxes and the swelling credit debt entered the mosques just to forget their quarrels at home and the uproarious cops and chabakounis, locust-like men who couldn't restrain themselves, even for a moment, from ravaging already precarious lands and minds. The poorer students became communists; or, if they couldn't, burned their notes and threw themselves into the nearest wadi where the last heads had been lopped clean off by the enslaved negros of ancient kings and cleverly preserved in salt, down in the *mellahs*, by the timid and downtrodden Jews, setting afloat a mirage of scintillations and shrill blood. Before long, the moon rose to power, expecting to remain there for some time. It bore children to perpetuate its atavistic lymph. Looming over any fanatical leader or loose cannon who viewed it as a means by which to accelerate typhoid, gangrene, and catastrophe of any kind for the benefit of those who knew perfectly well how to pull its strings and make its brilliance shine, without displacement or disintegration, at the stroke of midnight. This puppet-on-a-string moon would transform the landscape into an unprecedented abyss. The cops would burn away whoever wouldn't cast a smile in their direction or dared openly denounce them. They would douse the bodies not with gasoline but methylated spirits and disperse them to the crows out on the plains. The bourgeois themselves had been cast from the sphere of influence. They'd been replaced, on the sly, by the military and retired tirailleurs. The bourgeois dared not utter a word in opposition; their existence oozed from the *hammam*, and onto the open road, behind the wheel of the most recent model of car to hit the market. They traveled from place to place constantly, trying to forget their monetary expanse. Every now and then some nobody would forge the work of a revolutionary writer, forcing the king's defenses and its irony to its most grotesque point. Drivel—that's what their press was, crawling with grammatical errors and repressed desires! Perhaps even a purely erudite jealousy. Never did they make the slightest effort to free themselves from the moon. Just the opposite! Once in power, they arrested anyone walking around in too short of pants. To perpetuate their style of sectarianism, they felt the need to invent a moon of their own and do away with love-crazed spirits or any terrorist with an empty gut. They'd never forgotten they were

Andalusia's, and that they'd been converted against their will prior to having been driven from their homes by fanatically lucid Christians. The Christians wouldn't submit to the self-serving flights of fancy that defined the short-sighted kinglets and tradespeople carrying on their lives just hoping to get laid, *just one and I'm done! It's up inside you, woman, that I come alive.* Indeed, they would've been flushed out from the very eclipses they'd hoisted up! To begin, they massacred a great swathe of them! The ink in their books made the river run red. I understood that. I promised I wouldn't incinerate them but that I'd keep them on a leash, and at a distance, until after the revolution. I said such evil things to them. But can you call it evil if I've now revealed my identity? I'd resisted screwing their daughters, whose numerous taxi drivers would substantiate my claim that they'd always come to me begging for an orgasm. One had no tits whatsoever. I would take her up against the wall while my buddies listened to records. They told me I'd never have what it takes to love or to hate her. Sometimes I'd strip her down and make her roll around on the floor, feet against the entryway to the room. I wasn't afraid of the others seeing me go at it. The girl was hideous, but any last one of them would've given her a spin. Once we've got a hard-on, we're hardly thinking. We get off and get lost. How I would pound away at those labia. But I never hung around too long. Having cum, there I was, seeing myself off to some urgent business on the other side of town. It always left me feeling somewhat dirty. Something tantamount to a seal's slipping into its watery bath would ensue thereafter. Ah, cleanliness! Once I had her out of the picture, I was able to go quite some time without a shower. My skin was constantly cycling through hues. It blackened at first, then would illuminate in the blink of an eye and settle between a dusky gray and greasy green. Debt collectors could describe it with a mirror-like fidelity. At the time, I was holed up in a rather meager space in a rented-out room. My brother would pay me a visit twice a week. I had a lunatic for a roommate. I never brought any women back to this place. I worked my way through all the whorehouses in the older historic neighborhoods. I'd head there anytime I felt like it, even if I didn't have any money. When I got there, I'd ask the owner, who I'd managed to win over by getting shitfaced, to lend me the cash I needed. Usually, he'd do so without thinking. I can't say if it was my intelligence or my nerve he admired. Once inside, I'd give half the money to the girl and keep the other half to myself so that I'd be able to buy a couple rounds for the whoremongers on duty. One I'd really come to admire: Katatoès! He'd follow me around wherever I went. My father would refer to him as Numbskull-Full-of-Wine because he never seemed to sober up. To tell the truth, Katatoès was an absolute king, but don't go thinking some murderous vigilante or tyrant! The worst thing Katatoès ever took a knife to was a grapevine, and every now and then he'd churn out some poem inspired by a biblical passage or crime novel full of stiffs. We owed money to almost every dive in the neighborhood. Their proprietors would regularly stop by my house to shake me down for cash, but I'd likely be out again with Katatoès, in a place just across the street from theirs, no less. More often than not, we'd trash the place before even finishing our drinks. Because of the cash I'd burn through, new faces would gather around us. We'd raise a glass to each and every one of them, in unison. At that point, the political order had been either ramming itself down the people's throats, or else transforming itself into folkloric dances for the entertainment of shortchanged chancellors who'd yet to be reimbursed by The State. Whatever brambles of opposition may have existed at that point were mown down by secret police, and the political terrain raked entirely clean. Ben Barka hadn't yet left his earthly body, but a number of his comrades-in-arms had been mutilated, edged out, or simply left to rot down in the cellar of some private penitentiary. The State squandered its money on ammunition of every caliber, or on unscrupulous, low-grade henchmen. It doled out jobs to the greatest traitors of the colonial era, and the still less desirable flour-dredged Ouk-Ouks, who'd lubed up Vietnam with blood prior to the American penetration. General-Strong-Arm-of-Crime-and-Pestilence is one such example. And lo and behold he's remained there despite Gaulle's tug-of-war! Right now, he's worried about what, aside from a call for political restitution, might've taken root in that putrid compost: Now that the Yankees have planted their flag in the soil, laid claim to the leftover rank-and-file, and are sparing no expense upholding its Pestilence! Katatoès would always say of crime novels that they were the linguistic substance from which all literature began. He never wrote anything without a felt-tip pen—always in green ink. He'd thought it possible that one might change the course of history from within literature and claimed no text would go unnoticed or irritate any well-meaning souls, so long as it wasn't too clumsy or poorly wrought. He lived with his wife and two children—a five-year-old little girl and a tiny one only a few months old—in one of the street-level rooms of an estate that had once belonged to a European industrialist. His father kept a roof over their heads and provided for the entire family. Every day, around noon, I'd show up at his door. While his wife was busy suckling the kids, we'd pass a bottle back and forth looking for the bottom. We'd often lay out in the grass by the garden, discussing whatever came to mind, including my future travel plans. I told him that I'd be leaving the country soon, but I kept him in the dark about why. He thought I'd have what it takes to go forth and become a man of letters in a world otherwise infested by literary sharks. To tell the truth, he never wanted to see me getting involved in any political strife. He detested the king and his acolytes, going so far as to rage against every form of power there was, but it never resulted in more than grandiose indifference. He was of the mind that a writer was meant to forge a new world with his every act, but that he, himself, had no role to play in the political theater that was. Nevertheless, Katatoès loved to dive headlong into biblical history, which in of itself was little more than a sequence of politically motivated acts. He never went to bed without first reading one or two pages from *The New Testament*. Here and there, he'd manage to persuade me to lend his manuscripts an archeological eye, or, more honestly, a theological one. To do so, I told him I needed money, as well as the right texts, *I'll try and find you some books that mix religious thought with groundbreaking archaeological work. Otherwise, you won't get very far at all. Your age is getting the best of you, my friend. If you still have any remaining desire to be a writer, you'd better get at it.* He wanted, understandably, to collaborate with me as I reviewed his work; *We're gonna stick it to those petits-bourgeois, those hawkers, those paper-pushers, those intimistes and chariens, anyone getting their rocks off with poetry! Are we poets, yes or no?* After grabbing a bite to eat, Katatoès would drive me back to the office in his Volkswagen. I was still holding a steady job at the time. He'd drop me off in front of the so-called Social Security building, and I'd let him know that I'd see him again the next day. At the end of the workday, I'd go home. I'd plop myself down in front of an old typewriter that I called *The Hurricane* and start typing. Usually, I'd compose my texts without much prior thought; I was of the understanding that plans, notes, and other criteria necessary to the development of a novel would be of no use to me. I would write my way through the dark. Still, I'm inclined to admit that the books first took form in my brain before I put them to paper. I'd write with such speed that my own hand, grasping the pen, would be incapable of keeping up. More often than not, I'd spin out an epic poem and that would be that. One day, however, I must've struck just the right vein. I'd found myself totally bereft of productivity. I was absolutely incapable of putting my mind to anything, much less myself. But perhaps that's where the true creation begins. I'd already left crybaby sentimentalism in the dust, along with nostalgic thought of any kind. Mallarmé, too, had found himself in need of trudging through something like this. And yet how he continued to drone on and on! But a throw of the dice, and he was saved.

It was around that time that I'd already rejected all form, broken the normal metric—including that of vers libre. I listened only to the jerky rhythm of things. A creaky door could inspire me all the same as a man returning from a particularly daring venture. But I loved only the noise of *The Hurricane*. It seemed to me that each of its flailings deformed the word over the course of its impression as if it were the result of igneous fusion. I no longer had anything to say. I listened. But the day came when I hit a truly golden vein: Almost orgasmically, a text erupted, different than anything I'd written up to then: a rat-a-tat-tat of bullets followed by a rise of stifled howls. It was by way of this text I understood that I would have no choice but to commit myself, then and there, once and for all, to waging guerrilla linguistic warfare! However, soon I became completely closed off to others. I didn't even go into the office anymore. I'd sent a three-month medical certificate to my supervisor: an extraordinary sort. Go take a stroll through the neighborhood, he'd tell me, anytime I told him I was feeling down in the dumps. To tell you the truth, he probably still considers me something of a friend, but there's no way we'll ever see each other again. He understood, from very early on, that my sole employment was writing, and nothing but writing, writing with no end in sight, Someone may as well just nail you down to a table and give you a typewriter and some paper. You're an author! He knew perfectly well that my book would go on forever, that I was obsessed with getting it out, Fertilizer for the wilted conscience, that's what you're dredging up. And you're not coming out of that stable until it reeks. Indeed, a vast, bottomless stable—that's what he witnessed pumping through my veins, a stable condemned to be filled for as long as I'd be willing to empty it out. I was torn between lives. I loathed my origin, my parents, the world. I would stretch myself out under the sun, in front of the window in my room, sometimes even undressing myself, spreading my body across the sill like a lizard lapping up the sunlight. I had come to reject my relatives, my friends. The landlady would bring them to my door to no avail. Only Katatoès was allowed to step foot in my home. Our drunken stupors would begin every day at six o'clock sharp and wouldn't come to an end until somewhere around midnight or one in the morning. At the zenith of our stupor, we'd be screaming at one another. As things calmed down, we'd talk about language and history. But then some new argument even more off-the-rails than the last one would ensue. Katatoès never quite apprehended the organic function of words. He was conscious of their usage, but in a sense that smacked something of anachronism. Most of the phrases that came out of his mouth had been taken straight from the basic precepts of theology. Parables fished from the Bible, descriptions of spiritual turmoil, the omniscience of Christ—nonsense long buried by philosophers and dug back up to suit his needs at whatever moment. Once he even managed, somehow, to slip a book of verses under my nose, one which his brother, who'd died some time back after a botched operation, had published at his own expense. I opened my fly, rubbed my dick over the text's pages, struck the stature of a warrior prepared to do battle, and ripped the book into pieces right in front of Katatoès' face. He didn't even flinch, but I could see clearly that he was upset, and not with me but my gesture. I felt disarmed by his indifference. I don't know whether or not he was putting me on, but something had to be done! I screamed at him to get out. I couldn't stand to look at him. Get the hell out and don't ever come back! The next day, a mutual friend of ours, who'd spent the larger part of the last year being the social butterfly of the scene, reconciled us. It began in a hear-me-out-we-can't-separate-it-was-the-alcohol's-fault-we-drifted-apart-what'll-we-do-we'll-abstain-from-now-on-from-hitting-the-bottle-like-bottomless-holes, and ended in an absolutely marvelous drunken spree. The alcohol sent my meningitis into a tizzy, but I took it all in stride, or at least tried to. I was alright. We had ourselves one more drink in my bedroom, and then moved on to his place. His wife never joined in. And believe you me, we'd get in a lot of heated debates at his place, too. Mostly over politics. I came to think Katatoès might have felt more at ease if he'd just embraced his national identity, pure and simple. He'd made it through a long line of events that were well before my time. Had he known Lyautey? He wouldn't talk about it openly, but he knew Lyautey had been a feudalist. He never said anything to me about it. How did I know? I study my characters through and through. I see with X-ray vision. That's where real science comes in. And when it comes to history, you can't go wrong, especially when you stick to the facts. Katotoès didn't exactly have the same blood running through his veins that I did. His mother was Basque. Only his father was actually born here, this sterile rock I deign to call the country of Morocco. But the Basques, like the Imazighen, are men about whom we know nothing, or next to nothing. Colonized by one invader after the other, the one either exterminating or driving the other out—that's their cyclical state of affairs. Katatoès was reluctant to stir up trouble. While others were busy rioting, he was holed up in some bar. He could hear what was happening and he wouldn't move a muscle. He never spoke to me about the death of Cheikh el-Arab. Moreover, he never read the newspapers, other than those printed by a reactionary faction, to whom power was nothing more than something to be used to pull the wool over the people's eyes. His father had been able to procure French newspapers even in the utter worst of times, but he wouldn't share them with Katatoès, because he had a certain reverence for the outlaws in power, those who trembled with anger at the very thought of someone criticizing them with impunity. The type of maggots whose only concern was their bank accounts. The type whose only response to the events at hand was sending a squad of cops to spray down the square with bullets, to kidnap the students if they hadn't already been condemned to death in absentia—such was the case for Berrada, who'd managed to escape, though only after a very severe pummeling. The path is strewn with traps, but we can trust the people. It's through the work of the people that it'll be possible to preserve the seedling of the rebellion. To smuggle them into Algeria, where they might have the opportunity to acquire a passport, and maybe a little bit of money to help them continue their work. But will this heal a larger, ailing populace? No. We've got to stay focused on the scene of the crime. We've got to disinfect the vestibule itself, turn ourselves into pyromaniacal seers, and annihilate the royal loyalists and all the political shills that follow them. The rulers themselves have done nothing up to this moment but feel their way, precariously, along this mountain, this mountainous thing preparing to lay them into the ground and cover them over, this mountainous heap that is the people, the people-mountain, whose stomach growls, and turns the entirety of its strength inward, forming an unwitting collective, first through its dispersed crowds, and then through its communities united in arms; thusly, this people-mountain comes crashing down over kings of every sort, squashing the sources of feudalism, of indescribable smoke and mirrors, of threat after threat after threat haunting our dreams the moment we close our eyes. Death. In the face of powerlessness, we call out for death; that, or else we curl up into the fetal position and spare ourselves the whimpering; we die, silently; we stare out into the great unknown, and we expire. Katatoès wasn't capable of understanding things of that nature. He was one of those who was ripe—as Rimbaud might say—for fate's harvest. And indeed, fate would collect on its harvest: He passed away while he was reading and scribbling away at some quatrains, over an old invoice of his. Whenever I'd ventured to speak to him about the Black Struggle, of Césaire, or Malcolm X, he kept a tight lip. He'd prefer to speak of other things. Of a poet who tanned the hide of a goat, for example, just so he could write his little coldly calculated verse on it, in golden ink; or of a painter described to him by some schmoozing writer. Usually, it'd be some fakir who didn't belong in a world that would dare let its most precious herd go to waste. He didn't like to go out with anyone besides me.

He knew almost everything about my life, but never took much interest. He loved most of all to dream about the rear end of the ladies who hung out on the corner. He would seat himself down in the café terrace, downing red wine, and just stare, Ohh that one's really something. Check out this one—rotting from the inside out, I'm sure, like some long-ago felled tree; nothing down that rabbit-hole but green sap, piss, and dust. Shit not worthy of its name. Even syphilitic, maybe! I'd told him about my enraged and rage-worthy upbringing, at times quite calm, soothing, superb, but still, overall, somewhat abnormal: the repudiation of my mother, my father's sudden bouts with anger (he didn't drink, and he didn't smoke, but still—something was off). Katatoès would listen, unperturbed; my childhood, like almost everything else, mattered very little to him; that notwithstanding, my writing fascinated him, You'll never make it as a poet; you're bound to gain notoriety for your prose. In his Volkswagen, we'd travel back and forth across the city. I paid for gas, Katatoès having been out of work since the country's independence. I'd known him since secondary school. At the time, I'd abandoned my family: a runaway. For the second time. Katatoès was Chief of Personnel down at The Warehouse. He'd lean back in a chair in the middle of a large room, overseeing a group of men who'd finished last in their class, and who'd likely long abandoned their studies to muster more time to fuck around *(no pun intended)*. He loaned me a "sample" of a successful job letter. I copied it out and addressed it to the head of the factory. No response, despite Katatoès' recommendation. I was forced to take refuge with a cousin of mine. One who never shut up about my mother. There'd been a tension or rivalry from the start, one which supposedly went back quite a long way, far back through our ancestral lineage, but which nonetheless had been staunchly internalized, and had driven a wedge between my father and mother's family. This is why my cousin always had a drink on hand, whenever I felt the need. He ran a small mercantile he'd acquired from one of his former bosses who'd ended up an alcoholic. For lunch, we'd usually set something up in the back of the store. He made great tagines. I'd have some red wine while I was eating. He wouldn't drink a drop. He maintained a somewhat superficial clarity of mind, but I was never quite sure whether or not he drank. Until some of his teeth fell out, that is! Not only were his teeth covered in tartar, they'd been worn away, too. No doubt he must've gone on a serious bender from time to time. What's more, he must've made the rounds through a bevy of whores. He never said so, but I had my own special way of getting under his skin, past his silence. I abstained from asking any questions while he was busy taking care of customers. I took careful note of every little gesture he made: those lips of his that twisted so oddly when he smiled, that derisiveness and laughter he'd feign whenever the help swung by to get their pay. And I'd think to myself, that cousin of mine sure has a way of sweeping his Inveterate God, and all of his accompanying prophets, under the rug. Dreams and other fantasias perhaps not so much, since he let them crowd his mind. He'd often re-read *The Eternal Husband* and *Thus Spoke Zarathustra*. The Amazigh man, and many of the Imazighen, in fact, feel a sort of kinship with madmen and genies. They throw themselves at the world and its innumerable twists and turns, though this gives them a unique insight into all sorts of ways of life, all sorts of metamorphoses, and they end up with the ability to adapt with ease. They've the truth written across their brow, and they redraft their lives according to their taste, at which time they hand it over to the printer and await publication. It never quite yields the expected results, aside from the disgust it's designed to incite; instead it's rejected outright—inevitably—because it deals the powers that be a low-blow, because they refuse to be led any further down the path of their idiotic journey! And they'd never dare come face to face with their own failure… My cousin had gone out and purchased himself a hunting rifle. Which had necessitated the bribing one of His Majesty's ever-faithful civil servants, the needed permits slowly acquired one by one. He spent nine months in Casablanca and then the summer over at one of his places in the mountains. He spent most his time there hunting wild rabbits. His father always wore a tan and striped djellaba. This particular wardrobe choice gave him the appearance of a jackal. He was a goatherd. He was wealthy, but he never seemed to have a penny to spare. Before the French protectorate rose to power, he was viewed as just another one of those barbarians who deserved to get his skull crushed by the end of a rifle butt for setting foot in the region. At that time, the Imazighen suffered no king. They were quick on the trigger if they, or any of the many minions who served them, came into sight. Katatoès had two origins, but only in so far as man and beast could be said to share a common origin, variable in their eventual evolution; I'll leave myself out of it and simply say that Katatoès, instead of aligning himself squarely with the warrior tribe by taking up arms, continued to feed the lifestyle he'd grown accustomed to as he went on fooling himself. He wasn't the only one. An entire people has been annihilated in the drool of a single king stumbling drunkenly around and orchestrating firestorms wheresoever it pleases him, without somehow managing to incur any in return. The king disavows any internal labor or progress, yet he appropriates both if ever it should benefit his or his benevolent defenders' claim to power. He'll never observe Ramadan, and yet just as soon command others to do so. And every last one of them must witness, day after day, their voices disappear, alongside their strength and their power. They're so overwhelmed with aphasia that they've been moved to ecstasy before the very pestilence of the king's throat, ceaselessly erupting with sporadic nonsense. They only exist in and of themselves because they've fallen to their knees over an uneasy and grotesque fear. The fear of red-hot coals, under the control of theologians who've reimagined their formation a thousand times over and done their best to undermine the tongue of the Arab. Indeed, if only the Arabs hadn't doused their preordained-or-plagiarized-but-nowhere-to-be-found-God, whose wrath they've sermonized for ages, in the misty veneer of a world overflowing with gold; if only they'd taken their religion for what it was, the discarded spoils of a bloody feast served up over a sandy wasteland, no more than a literary and metaphysical miscellany, then indeed, the Arabs might've given God the Non-Existent an excuse to be, along with every last anchorite-wrought-sword-of-a-beard!

Moreso than anything else, I was taught fear—transfixed by it. Fear was everywhere. In my own house, inlaid in who or whatever came my way; fear, disguised by silhouette, heading down every street corner: the very intersection of the abyss! Unassuming fear. I stared that fear down, face to face, vowing to tear limb from limb any god who'd so much as try spreading it from impressionable mind to impressionable mind. Now I've arrived at the sum-totality of that anger. I say to myself, Whenever you feel that fear may have lashed you down, go ahead—lash out. And that's just it, that's exactly what every last person in this world—every last person who sees nothing but the image of a cop's nightstick seared into memory the moment they close their eyes, about to come down on the world at any given second—should do! I've gone so far as to put death at the helm. Death, who stumbles back and forth and drinks himself into a stupor before fear's eyes. I lashed out at Death, let it slither down my throat, and then vomited it back up again! It wasn't so disgusting a thing. It actually languished there for a while, but still, fear remained fear, in that it might resurface as something far more gruesome. My vomit, run red after having digested so many torrential horrors and precalculated atrocities, forced the fear to protrude from my eye like a screwworm larva unscrewing up and out of a giant pile of shit.

FEAR ME, I AM YOUR FATHER!

FEAR GOD! In short,

FEAR!

This is the intricacy from which my life manifests itself. I've never rid myself of it. This fear has woven itself into my nightly web. It draws itself up over my body and wraps itself around my cerebral membrane. It screws its way through my skull and disappears somewhere in my hair, only to circle back and suspend itself, once again, before my eyes—unmoving, grotesque, and cruel. THE KING—NOTHING BUT ANOTHER NAME FOR EXISTING CENTURIES WITHOUT COMING INTO CONSCIOUSNESS, FOR TURNING YOUR BACK ON A WHOLE GENERATION OF SKULL-PEELED CHILDREN, AND THEN DISAPPEARING INTO THE CLOUDY NOTHINGNESS OF DUST.

What follows is a sample from a much longer list of your lawless endeavors. In this requisitory, you shall not be called to question, and if you are, no one shall be able to entirely make out your design; you shall scarcely play any role whatsoever. In the following, what shall be brought into question is a particular veneer of proceedings, one which composes men from constituent lines thereby, taking them as the sum of their parts. You shall see no more than two resulting outlines; and both shall serve (or shall symbolize, presenting themselves against white space) two distinct purposes, while not necessarily proceeding in opposition to one another. In the center, a flat line, curved indefinitely, nonetheless with incredible precision; eye-catching, in other words. It is black and incisive. It meanders, wriggles around until it overflows its area of operation. As it designs its course, a manifold multiplicitousness emerges: exceptionally brutal and significant, but at the same time present only in absentia, on account of the raw features which bring it into being, scarcely even sketched out; wonderfully terse, nevertheless; articulate, even. The focal point, its medium (?), is what feeds their weakness, while revealing none; this is what *thinks* and then organizes them. This is theater in so far as it shall become that which is most instantaneously engrossing. Here, we must consider the Act, the multi-faceted Movement, The Gesture and The Word, as potentially materializable action, not as an object one feels compelled to enter into dialogue with. The canvas, which up to the present moment has been no more than a point of departure, shall impress the forms invading it with an unstable character and a continual displacement, perceptible and easily distinguishable at first glance, so that the reader need only look toward or touch upon this or that character in order to know their more secretive nature. The same shall hold true of the instability and mayhem that they are intended to provoke.

PROLOGUE

Gunshots. Silence. Rustling.
The King speaks from backstage.

THE KING

These burgeoning conspiracies are closing in around my brain, but who dares pit themselves against me; tell me that, huh, who dares? Enough! Lapdogs, hired guns, and corrupted holy men are the only guerrillas I need! Right now, my soldiers are out on every street, cleansing the city of every last remnant of liberty, one I could just as easily have smothered in flames.

Boots shuffling. Gunshots. Screams.
Darkness. Silence.
The King continues to speak.

The throne, huh, my throne, that's what you want, isn't it? It's over. Keep that in mind; I'm no small-time hustler. Watch me close down the hospitals, you'll all be dead, and I'll be dancing upon your graves. My brilliance amounts to more, so much more, than any sunlight your ancestors handed down to you, ha! But this sun, here, this sunlight encompasses my country! And I'll drive it straight through your spine like a Grand Cross, and while you're dying in some deeply-entrenched ditch, somewhere, along with all the other stray dogs, I'll be indulging myself, alone, skirting my way around the last table ever set, at the very threshold of hell.

Go back to sleep, my people, doodle away in your books, nibble the ends of your pencils; my ancestors were versed in taking heads. I'm looking out for you; I am you, but you've been fussing around too much to notice that your papa's been looking over your shoulder this entire time, as the great famine seizes upon your home, leaving an infestation of pests in its wake.

Applause from backstage.

BANDEROLE I

Light.
A banderole is unfurled, across which some writing can be read.

THE PEOPLE'S PUTREFACTION MORE THAN ANYTHING ELSE OWES TO HIS UNWAVERING POLICY OF PLEDGING OBEDIENCE LIKE HIS ANCESTORS BEFORE HIM TO MONSTERS WHO ARE BUT MEN BORN IN SOME FAR-OFF LAND BUT WHO NEVERTHELESS LEAVE AN IMPRESSION MORE STRIKING THAN A BOUQUET OF FIRE IN THE MOUTH OF A SALTIMBANQUE!

MOVEMENT I

A room in pure Moorish style. Blue mosaics in some areas, and up on the ceiling, the inscription "Ilah," "Allah," in Arab characters.

To the right of the backstage, against the wall, a bust of the star of the music hall.

In the center of the stage, a washbasin.

Two black servants circle around, carrying thuribles, whose contents they shake before emptying them into the washbasin.

Just as they leave, two new characters enter the stage.

The King and the Imam.

Both seem agitated. Their movements are chaotic.

They circle the stage, one after the other.

Then they stop, abruptly, as if to speak with one another.

At first, it seems as though a fight is about to ensue.

But a gunshot from backstage stops them dead in their tracks.

THE KING

The script. Ah, here it is, the script. They're in a frenzy out there, ready to tear it all down—and us along with it. Ah, yes, the script, here goes:

"We the propagator of the sacred order,
"We who have reinforced the divine order,
"We the…

He reflects.

god of the land…

THE IMAM

Why land and not heavens? You are divine, after all.

THE KING

"God of the land!

A beat.

"We who have chopped off the heads,
"dispossessed…

THE IMAN

It's upside down. Let's begin again.

THE KING, *impatient*

Just tell me what I need to tell them already.

A beat.

The people love words they don't understand. Especially when you stick your foot in your mouth; don't make me waste my time on this. I'm going to need a good round in my harem as soon as we're done. Quickly now.

The Imam addresses the King as if an unruly schoolboy.

THE IMAM

You've done press conferences in French, but you don't speak a lick of Arabic.

A beat.

Behold, this is exactly what they need to hear:

"We, the bearer of woes from a dead god inside this bloody Being.

The King slaps him.

Ah, got it. No bearer of woes. My mistake. Won't happen again.

THE KING, *whining and stamping his feet*

Your script!

THE IMAM

Blood's Being! Shit! It's Aïssa we're dealing with here. Jesus. Let's try to avoid that kind of propaganda, otherwise sooner or later we'll all be double-crossing each other. How about this: "We who carry out the work of Time."

THE KING, *conciliatory*

No, no, no! I'm begging you—get to the point, already. You've got to sell the very lifeblood to a people this stupid.

Gunshots from backstage.
Noise.
Then a long drawn out groan, cut off only by the noise of cannon-fire.

THE IMAM, *trembling*

Huh, what's going on out there? Ah, "We who complicate the lives of illiterate people..."

A beat.

Sir, I must confess that I'm beginning to think I've had my fill of power.

THE KING *slaps the Imam, scolding him*

Write the speech right this instant, or else I'll have you thrown in prison!

THE IMAM, *weeping*

With nothing to show for it! We are the... What! What are we?

Gone to shit, that's what!

THE KING, *yells*

Idiot!

Sarcastically.

I'm going to have your head chopped off, in traditional fashion.

THE IMAM, *still trembling*

Execution-style? Were you not already planning on that, regardless? No, I'd prefer not to have my head swinging from ghetto walls. No, no, no—Your Majesty—I've just thought of something more original. An ancient parchment which bears the insignia of Ali Baba. No, wait, the insignia and seal of Ali-The-Caliph; that's who.

A beat.

The Imam raises his hand, once again playing the role of school master.

Of course it's essential that you learn this script by heart, just as soon as I've made some historical tweaks. It's… Listen to this…

"The King of Babylon set a trap for Us, and yet…"

THE KING, *boiling over with rage*

Filthy mystic! What've I to do with traps or the King of Babylon! Get me that finalized script, or else!

THE IMAM

I'm literally overflowing with ideas. Let's change it all; this script is going to be something else altogether, one that…

THE KING

Get on with it!

THE IMAM

You're going to have to show our adversaries—measly foreigners, as far as we're concerned—just what we're capable of. Errrm, uhh… Just what you're capable of, Your Majesty. Yes, you, it is you who govern by way of the word, written and spoken. You grasp the impact of a passionate speech. Err… Yes, just wait until you get a load of this script after it's rewritten; it's bound to be the greatest speech of the year. When first our time came to be, it was only those like you—poets like you—who could even dream of seizing and securing power. You remember the Andalusian court, don't you?

THE KING, *more and more impatient*

Give me that script already!

THE IMAM

I… I don't have it on me. Heh…

He trembles.

It's in my head.

Darkness.

Gunshots backstage.

The King stomps at the ground with his feet.

He drags the Imam toward the exit, all the while muttering monosyllabic words such as "beh, agh. Grr…"

Once backstage he lets out a terrifying scream resembling something like a woman climaxing.

Black. Silence.

MOVEMENT II

A room furnished with a sofa bed and a table.
On the table is a carafe of water.
Red light over the stage.
Three people, El Arab, Mehdi, and an undercover police officer are seated on barstools.
A wind from backstage.
Then footsteps.

MEHDI, *calmly*

Where do mathematics lead?

EL ARAB, *irritably*

Toward the assimilation of History, toward the true assimilation of History.

THE POLICE OFFICER

I didn't come here to talk numbers, I came here to warn you about the cops. In a little while, a buncha cops—ones far more serious than I—are gonna be busting straight through that door. And you'd better be ready.

MEHDI *grows restless.*

Let's go! I don't think we should wait around any longer, c'mon, let's get out of here.

He leaves.

EL ARAB, *sarcastically*

Ah! Intellectuals!

He takes a pistol out of his pocket.
Peers down the barrel and kisses it, affectionately.

As far as I'm concerned, you're the only one I can count on to liberate the people. And rest assured, I will liberate my people!

THE POLICE OFFICER
You did, already—it just wasn't enough; the sharks and kings are busy turning the country's independence into a blood-soaked parody. By the way, you should get outta here; they're on their way, right now, with reinforcements, they're gonna kill you, they…

EL ARAB
They don't even know I'm here. The only one who knew is a friend; how could he dare turn his back on me, eh?

THE POLICE OFFICER
He did. You're a dead man. Best not stick around much longer, or else you can kiss your life and the people's liberation goodbye.

Gunshots off-stage.

EL ARAB *takes a whiff of his pistol.*
And away we go! Let's get this party started.

He fires a few times towards the backstage.
The police officer pulls out his revolver and runs off.
Some time in darkness.
Gunshots. Vehicle noise.
Then some light.
A street can just barely be distinguished, along with a corpse lying in a corner.
A man takes a whiff of his pistol, and then disappears.

MOVEMENT III

The King and the Iman are standing before the bourgeois assembly.

THE KING, *to the Bourgeois*

Go ahead, laugh! This swine over here told me he'd somehow gotten his hands on a speech signed by Ali-The-Caliph himself. And the minute I express any interest whatsoever, he says he doesn't have it, that he merely knows *of* it. He must have read about it in one of his dusty old theological tomes. In any case, it's nothing that hasn't been heard before. What I need is something new! I must have something new, or else I risk falling out of the people's good graces!

A beat.

Laugh it up at his expense. Do what you will to him. We're about to find ourselves in some real deep shit, and it's all because of him!

The Bourgeois smack the Imam around. But not one of them seems to be enjoying themselves.

THE KING

You're nothing but a bunch of talking heads! Live a little!

THE IMAM

Mercy, I beg you! I've got the script; I swear to you I've got it.

THE BOURGEOIS, *to the King*

This is no laughing matter; he is nothing but an ignoramus!

To the Imam and the King.

What are you trying to do, play right into the hands of our adversaries?

THE KING

Me? Never!

ONE OF THE BOURGEOIS, *to the King*

You should have let them take over to begin with, or at least let them in on the government. After all, you are only king because *we* say it is so. It remains a matter of shared interest—of immediate and long-term investments. We are here to stay, and as such we are taking this opportunity to warn you once again: The situation into which you have embroiled us cannot go on a moment longer.

A beat.

And if it does, it is sure to be '89 all over again, right here.

THE BOURGEOIS, *together*

We shall wait until Year 1—1989, that is—before cutting your head off.

A member of the Bourgeois rings a bell.
In comes one of their lackeys.

THE BOURGEOIS

Bring us some scotch! And you are to serve not one drop to the King. We must ensure that he keeps a clear head.

To his fellow bourgeois.

We need a script worthy of its name: an elegant speech. Nothing less.

He redirects his attention to the Lackey, who hasn't moved.

Just what are you waiting for?

THE LACKEY

Right away, right away.

THE KING, *pacing in circles around the stage*

I'm no Eastern king. The sort of king you'd no doubt cherish having under your thumb. I am Head of State, not some Louis XVI! Not an overseer of locks and chains! I made my way through the university. But afterwards, I made my own way, in voluntarily exile, where I grew more and more solitary, solitary as a yeti. Indeed, those who got too close to me around that time I've since had exterminated. Moving forward, I've raised my own inner circle of cut-throats and sharpshooters; and on the strongest drug conceivable: the almighty dollar! But I've still got one or two more tricks left up my sleeve, hence my prestigious name…

THE BOURGEOIS

Rogue!

THE KING

Shut your despicable mouths! Might I remind you, you don't so much as exist without me. Your wealth is worthless anywhere else. Rest assured, no one outside the country would even come near it.

THE IMAM

Go on, Sire.

THE BOURGEOIS, *to one another*

Who will speak for us?

A BOURGEOIS

I will. He may as well hear what we all are thinking.

He turns to the King.

Our wealth? It is thanks to our wealth that you remain alive. Only our wealth will be able to save you from your inevitable overthrow someday. Quit with your temper tantrum. All we are asking for is that you be a monarch worthy of representing us. Moreover, you could perhaps conduct yourself with a little grace in front of the people, not to mention foreign nations.

A beat.

Furthermore, we shall not ignore the fact that you have been devoting your foremost attention to the army. What is to become of us in a year or two from now? What do you plan to do, send us into exile?

A beat.

Above all else you are hoping and praying that we stay put, to play a part in the massacres that you plan to commit using those military lowlifes of yours.

Constantly turning away from him, the King stops, from time to time, to examine the walls.

THE KING

How at ease you seem, vomiting your bile—please, don't hold anything back now.

THE IMAM, *nervously*

Sire, you're not just going to let him get away with that, are you?

THE KING

Absolutely not!

He gazes up at the ceiling. A crystalline star, serving as a chandelier.

Absolutely not! I refuse to respond to questions put up by the bourgeois, whose only ambition is to find ways of benefitting from my reign. They're up in arms now, sure, but all that aside, they're infinitely more cowardly than they appear. They're nothing but children!

He fixes his gaze on the Bourgeois.

Going on and on like some sniveling little brat isn't a good look for you! You're not so innocent yourselves! I'm far more concerned about what the students are up to. How they lick the ends of their pens with such purpose—I suppose ink's enough to give the people its fill. Genetically speaking, you bourgeois amount to nothing. Bunch of would-be abortions! Your monetary delusions are nothing compared to what the students are doing. Theirs is an organic—however devil-may-care—experiment. Your thirst for power is, at one and the same time, outlandishly spiteful and pitiable. It's eating its way through your own pathetic cerebellum, not mine. You don't need a throne; what you need is your head cracked open, and a stick of dynamite rammed up your ass! Maybe that's the way to get the hereditary importance of a king through your thick skulls!

In comes the Lackey, whose arrival to serve the Bourgeois their scotch has momentarily shifted the room's attention.

The King continues, regardless.

I'm not here to entertain you, nor to bestow you with the ripened fruit of my labors. You are hereby prohibited from ever stepping foot in here again. My salons are designed for poets and savants. Not the flabby bodies of the bourgeois. From now on, and quite in line with the conclusions drawn from this meeting, you shall have nothing further to contribute to my estate. I shall leave you to your own devices. Enjoy paying the highest tax rates I can muster. I have no fear of your childish threats. My ideology remains intact.

THE BOURGEOIS, *after talking among themselves for a moment*

Your Majesty, rest assured, your ancestors were no less cruel to us than you.

THE KING, *raising his voice*

I'm speaking! Sure, you've mucked things up—but know this: It is I who am capable of steering things back to normal. The sharpest of the anti-bourgeois and anti-revolutionary cutthroats are about to see what this brain of mine can really do. Things your order's craftsmen could never imagine, things you've never seen in your wildest dreams!

A beat.

This putrid stench that I fear, it's nothing to do with the bourgeoisie.

To the Lackey.

Go and tell the General that I've got a plan in mind that will take care of the bourgeoisie once and for all.

The Lackey bows to the King, then exits the stage.

THE IMAM, *empathetic.*

You and I are of one mind, Your Majesty. You are the loveliest of lights in the dark, and the greatest that ever deigned to cast its rays down upon us, to bathe us in a sweet paradise, and allow us to gaze, grotesque as any death, into the blue hole of hell.

THE KING, *to the Imam*

Shut up.

He points toward the Bourgeois, who are busy consulting with one another just off-stage.

These fools want us morally crippled. Let's make sure we get rid of them before the first cannon heralds the fast.

A beat.

They deny me all of life's greatest pleasures. Every last one! They know exactly what they're doing. They're even after my women. How dare they! If I so much as touch one of their scotches, they'll have photographers swarming me in a second. Let's not even think about where that road leads. And afterwards I'll just end up conceding to them, as usual.

A beat.

Why don't they go fuck their mothers, all of them! No self-respecting king bows down to the rich, or cops. You know this.

The Lackey returns.

THE LACKEY

It's done, Sire.

THE KING

Take these men outside. Sequester them to the hallway. No, to the antechamber. The General will deal with them.

The Lackey sees to the exit of the Bourgeois. He follows. The King stays behind with the Imam.

THE KING

Quickly, the speech.

THE IMAM

Wait. We've got to…

The same lackey comes back in again.

THE LACKEY, *to the King*

The General has expelled the gentlemen.

THE KING

Who cares. Where's the tape-recorder?

THE LACKEY

It's right there, I'll set everything up.

THE KING

Good.

To the Imam.

You'll do the speech. A difficult task, but an exercise in royal responsibility! It's late; by now we should be in Paris, or London, a club somewhere.

A beat. The Lackey sets up the tape-recorder and then leaves.

Don't mince words; critique all parties involved, even our own. Also be sure to work in the death of my father along the way, the people being the bunch of softies they are. What else is new! Between you and I, my father was more of a transitionary type of king. Make it seem as though the bourgeois are on their hands and knees. Grant amnesty—verbally—to no one, except for revolutionaries who've been exiled, or those currently in jail. I've no intention whatsoever of granting freedom to the former, nor any pardon to the latter. They're nothing but potential assassins in the making, driven by possessive instincts whose point of origin I can't even begin to comprehend.

A beat.

Give the students a good tongue-lashing. Tell the unemployed to enroll in the army. Assure every last one of them that they'll benefit from my clemency and understanding. Tell the students that they will receive an educational grant if they agree to my terms. Say that I am a decent man, a very humble being, a true socialist and a former student revolutionary. Whatever you do, mention nothing of my trouble with the chancelleries.

A beat.

Finally, make sure that God is predominant, throughout every last sentence of the speech, and that he shines his light from on high.

THE IMAM

Hey, what about the El Arab business?

THE KING

No, no, don't mention him.

He leaves, murmuring.

What an idiot!

Black.
Commotion from backstage.

MOVEMENT IV

A reception room in the royal palace.
Tables and chairs on both sides.
Superior officers, dignitaries, ministers, ladies, lackeys.
The groups are chatting, congratulating one another.
Spotlight on three people only, all standing in the center of the stage.
A general, a captain, and one lavishly dressed lady.
Only the silhouette of others can be seen.

THE GENERAL

The King is beginning to depend more and more upon the bourgeoisie.

THE CAPTAIN

Merely for the sake of appearances. He knows our soldiers could do him in at any moment. The King is our slave, nothing more.

THE LADY

You're wrong. The King depends upon the people, even if he may, from time to time, humiliate them. The people love a good tussle. The King need only give the order and his people will rise up against you.

Laughter, chamber music, noise from backstage.

THE CAPTAIN

That does it! I'm just as smart as any of you; so why aren't I receiving the credit I deserve?

THE GENERAL

I've been at this a lot longer than you have, yet you don't see me asking for one thing in return. My rank is good enough. It's conceivable that I could convince the King to grant me a higher title or some key position in the government, but I've no desire. As far as nations go, we're still on the younger side. Still dependent on those abroad. Take it easy for once; let's not get too ahead of ourselves.

THE CAPTAIN

I'm being sent abroad to sort out this mess because of you. Sure, you may outrank me; still, you should have had the courage to stand up to your accusers in the first place. You certainly made short work of the bourgeoisie, but answer me this: Just how many military heroes or innocent bystanders are you willing to sacrifice to maintain your image?

THE GENERAL

That all depends on the King. It's out of my hands.

THE LADY, *to the General*

He's young, that's clear enough. But you—you, on the other hand, are a seasoned military man. A veteran of the colonial times. Perhaps that's the reason you can't seem to muster a personal opinion on the matter. An impartial warrior—a blind warrior—that's what you are!

THE GENERAL, *to the Lady*

I come from an impoverished family. I made a commitment to the colonial army so that I might scrape together a living for my mother and sister. My mother is dead. My sister no longer depends on me. It's possible she may even be in opposition to the monarchy now. If that's the case, and if someone were to order it, I'd shut her up just as soon as anyone else.

To the Captain.

You're a watchman; it's essential you remain loyal to your superiors. Never step out of line. And never show support for the opposition.

A beat.

Any demonstration of support for the civilian or military resistance will be regarded as a subversive act. Let it be known, then, that any subversive act will be nipped in the bud.

THE CAPTAIN

Ah, so that's it, it's me you've chosen to make an example of. You've sent me straight into the lion's den. Why not just throw me into one of your prisons? I've exposed myself to the worst accusations imaginable. They gave me a hundred lashings! What a joke; and still, I was immediately promoted to Captain right after. Ah! What a joke. I've swallowed my pride as an officer; all to please you, to clean up your own dirty laundry.

A beat.

And now, what're you gonna…

The Lady cuts him off.

THE LADY

Shh, the King's on his way.

Preceded by the General-Minister-of-the-Interior, the King enters.
Light over the entire scene.

THE GENERAL-MINSTER-OF-THE-INTERIOR,
to the attendees

Subordinates, eminent subjects of His Majesty, ladies of honor, gentlemen ministers. I have an announcement to make: A general strike has just been broken. However, some cities in the kingdom still teem with activity, and we can expect a large-scale action if, in the next twenty-four hours, our soldiers and our armored vehicles do not put an end to it. At this current time, our troops and our tanks are blocking every vital entryway to the center of the capital and making sure that nothing unbecoming befalls our residents from abroad. The royal palace and our villas are not in danger! His Majesty has kept a close eye on our economic capital from aboard his helicopter. He has given the order to open fire only after having devoted considerable thought to the current situation. As supreme leader of the army and head of the State, he could hardly do otherwise. Long live the King and long live the fatherland!

He bows down slavishly before the King.

May God grant our Master long life!

THE KING

There shall be no mention of the ongoing riots in the speech I am about to give. The people must remain ignorant to any naysayers or opposition to the progressive forces of the country—our own, needless to say. Long have we grappled with different oppositional factions; nevertheless, we've maintained the upper hand in remaining more clear-headed than any of the leaders of those organizations.

A beat.

My speech is no common tirade anymore. Listen up!

Total silence.
The King seats himself in front of the help.
He pours himself a glass of scotch, swallowing it in one gulp.
He pours a second and holds it out in front of him.
Then, he removes a double leaflet from the inner pocket of his tunic.
Just then, whispers can be heard from backstage.
The King demands silence.
Finally, he begins to recite his speech.

THE KING

"We, the bearers of God's permanent grace, of his prophet and that of our ancestors, of a flawless power which is envied by the infidels and the unstable,

"We who have fought many years against the establishment of colonialism and organized crime, in our lands, and in our consciences,

"Against the makers of massacres and misery, all the wheelers and dealers and antihistorical demons!

"We Alone,

"who have contested every demagogic form of power, and who have steered this Vessel known as our Kingdom so very magnificently,

"We, the bejeweled, without whom the situation would surely return to its former state of grave precariousness!

"We who listen only to our hearts and refuse to bend the rule of law which has been passed down to us through centuries,

"We, the Chosen Ones,

"have determined the monarchy to be the sole good of the people, and that the conspirators, as well as other delinquents, are better off elsewhere.

"We have closed the doors to our prisons; by which I mean those in which some of our greatest heroes have awaited their fate.

"We have given everything in our possession to the learned dignitaries we are assisting in the perilous tasks set out before us.

"We welcome in millions of our overseas allies, every year, with open arms.

"Our soldiers would never dream of issuing a complaint in regard to their compensation. On the contrary, it is thanks to our gold that the evening establishments bid them a warm welcome and conduct their business according to the strictest letter of the law. Granted, however, some of our soldiers still frequent seedy hotels, shabby cafes, and whorehouses forbidden by the Qur'an. Those soldiers are clawing for a great nostalgia, for a time of imperialists and colonists, and they are out to destroy themselves, much to the benefit of the rebels. We shall not consider them good soldiers, despite them having proven their courage during the border wars.

A beat.

"We hereby certify, therefore, that the right to exercise the full extent of our power shall, most fortunately, be placed in no one's hands but our own!

Applause and hooting.

"We Alone can steer our Vessel to fortune!

"We Alone have seen to it that the kingdom is endowed with research facilities and nationalized factories!

"We alone ask that the communists share their resources with us in order to build up our blockades.

"The price of sugar has risen due to our curtailed trade with Cuba! Leave Cuba to the third world! We have nothing in common with communists of their sort!

"We Alone, despite the combined efforts of the students and other such madmen, have inscribed the exact same will of the people's contestations straight into the annals of the public works! Let the workers hunt their bosses down. It's all the same to us! It's the people upon whom all rights shall be bestowed!

“We shall resolve every problem in due time, though it require a modicum of patience.

A beat.

“Duty, above all else.

“May this nation fulfill its territorial destiny! In several months, we shall declare war upon our neighboring states!

“Dear People,

“We have everything it takes for a thousand years’ reign, without any need of colluding with foreign nations. We have such armed forces that any abroad who choose to set their sights on us shall tremble with fear. At our borders, as well as the thresholds of our very abodes, evil spirits shall shudder at the very prospect of appearing before Us.

A beat.

“Dear People,

“We have everything it takes to provide you with a life of peace. Our constitution is being amended as we speak. We thought it necessary to redraft it entirely, seeing as some of its finer points have yet to be tried and tested. Rest assured, it shall be in accordance with your needs and your desires.

A beat.

“Dear People,

“Obey none but your faith and the traditions of Ramadan! Our enemies are fooling no one. We shall slaughter them all, one after the other. If they should choose to observe Ramadan, they shall be admitted and counted among us, once again, as our brothers; at long last, they shall come to see the strength and the will of the popular masses!

"May God remain the unrivalled standard of our glorious kingdom!"

Applause once again, followed by more hooting.

MOVEMENT V

In a café.
Three people. Two unemployed men and a waiter.
The waiter stands behind the bar. He is sipping tea.
The two unemployed men have nothing.
Above the bar, on a large shelf, a television set.
On the screen of the device one can observe the out-of-focus image of the King finishing the last words of his speech.

THE KING

"May God remain the unrivalled standard of our glorious kingdom!"

Pop music.
One of the unemployed men bursts into laughter.

UNEMPLOYED MAN ONE

Ha ha ha ha ha! Can you believe this pile of shit!? More than a pile of shit, even; shit spewing from every orifice he's got, ha ha ha!

UNEMPLOYED MAN TWO, *to the Café Waiter*

How 'bout a drink, we're good for it.

THE CAFÉ WAITER

No chance, lazyasses! Nah, no chance in hell!

UNEMPLOYED MAN ONE

Funny country, isn't it! Those who don't know a thing about my situation care little about the overall situation. You won't find me fasting like the old days; that's already my entire life—one never-ending fast. They can all go fuck themselves! The cops roughed me up on the way outta the factory, and the boss told me never to come back. It's those pig sonsofbitches who put pressure on him. And why? Because I'm registered with the union, that's why, and I'm fighting for a little justice and the right to unionize. After the strike, the boss closed down the factory, entirely; just left. Didn't even bother selling the thing. The union didn't want anything to do with it. Every morning I make the trip from the slums to the local head's office. He won't see me. Every day I'm told the same thing: that he's out; that, or he's in prison.

THE CAFÉ WAITER

That's none of my business!

UNEMPLOYED MAN TWO

Me, I'm still working two hours a week. Doing what my wife did before Independence: cleaning the house of the King's attorney. He pays next to nothing! How could anyone be that stingy? Makes you wonder what he's doing with all that money. Ah, but I've got some idea: he's got mistresses around here—and over in Paris, too. That's where all the money in the country goes.

THE CAFÉ WAITER

Get outta here! Go spout your politics somewhere else!

UNEMPLOYED MAN ONE

Shit, the cops!

Two agents and a police sergeant enter.

THE POLICE SERGEANT, *to the Café Waiter*

How about a round of drinks? C'mon, c'mon—we're in a hurry. Hey, who's this sad sack of shit drinking with you? What're these two assholes doing here?

THE CAFÉ WAITER, *hesitating*

They were watching the television. And uh, ah… And talking

politics. And ah, uh… Neither of 'em have got much sense for politics, let alone their tabs. The owner's gonna close up shop if this keeps up—and then I'll be out on my ass too. The last thing I wanna be is a deadbeat like them… Ugh!

THE POLICE SERGEANT

Politics! These deadbeats talking politics! We don't need anyone sitting around twiddling their thumbs. The King would prefer you settle down elsewhere. How about France?—of course, there won't be much left to see, if push comes to shove. You've got no business in our town.

UNEMPLOYED MAN ONE

Throw me in jail! I've got kids, and nothing to feed them. The price of sugar has already skyrocketed; don't even get me started on tea! The grocers refuse to give me anything more on credit. The baker refuses to lend me any more flour. One single sack is all I've got left, and even that's laced with rat shit. It's all my kids and I have been eating. And the butcher? Don't even think about it! I owe him too much already. It's only a matter of time until he starts complaining too.

A beat.

But oh, the cops, they're doing just fine. They're doing very, very fine. You're all a bunch of rats. It's all going to the cops, isn't it? Go ahead, then, throw me in jail, my rugrats too, teach me, teach me how to be a cop!

THE POLICE SERGEANT

Just another deadbeat trying to get his fill, eh? You're nothing more than an enemy of the people.

He walks up to Unemployed Man One, slaps him with all his strength.

Nothing but an enemy, huh, isn't that right? Nothing but a dirty, low-down enemy! And the message, I presume, was clear to you on the television!

A beat.

Unemployed Man One does not move.

An enemy of the people! If I was the government, I would… Hmph! I'm just a cop, trying to make my way. C'mon, let's get him over to the station!

The agents take Unemployed Man One away.

THE CAFÉ WAITER

What about the other one?

THE POLICE SERGEANT

You—shut your mouth. We'll be back.

A beat.

To close up shop.

MOVEMENT VI

Friday.

A flurry of activity at the entryway to the mausoleum.

The King has not yet been announced, but black guards are holding up a portrait of him, exhibiting it for public view.

Noise. Horns from afar.

Strangely tense atmosphere.

Generals, dignitaries, armed soldiers.

The soldiers are outfitted for combat.

They rally around their superiors, weapons pointed towards the crowds of people who are waving black handkerchiefs and clutching envelopes in their hands.

The King passes by on a white horse.

The crowd notices him, yet they remain indifferent.

A VOICE FROM THE LOUDSPEAKER

The King who accepts us generously into his heart now graces us with his presence. Not only is he submitting to a custom he holds near and dear, he is allowing us to take up a seat in his benevolent light.

A VOICE FROM THE CROWD

The King just went by. Anyone see him? Who here saw the King? I didn't. How condescending for him to hide; he's just trying to avoid our accusatory gazes. Now that he knows we want him out. His father was much more forward, though more conniving, I'll admit. His father would never have hidden from us though.

A beat.

I only saw him once. At the time, I remember how focused I was on his ear, his left ear, which I kept a close eye on, the entire time he was delivering his speech. It gleamed in the sunlight. The King's ear was so very odd. It was unlike the ear of any other man… Uh, eh, where was I?

Laughter.

Oh yes, that's right, his ear. His son could never really measure up to that ear of his father's. Nevertheless, he did have the same body, the same throne, the same palace. I have to say, though, his chair was a real nasty sight.

Laughter.

And to think that he'd sometimes invite us over!

A VOICE FROM THE LOUDSPEAKER

The King does not stand with those who refuse to remember the bloody strikes which almost endangered the well-being of the people and their democracy. The King does not stand with those who refuse to remember the religious establishments which were endorsed by his absolute omnipotence. May it please God! Even he wept to learn that the rebels laid siege upon the holy men and the palace. Our King must be our guide. It is he who steers the vessel. He is the one true representative of the prophet's family. May it please God that he seeks no reward for his personal efforts! May he know your will better than yourselves! May our allies across the Atlantic—who daily hold our thoughts and our prayers, not merely because of their technological prowess, but also their military prowess, which they spread across the entire world, against communist aggressors and obscurantists of all kinds—may these allies of ours across the Atlantic take heed of our renewed oath of goodwill, through the voice of God, addressing them as our Omnipotent Kingdom! Along the borders, as through our homes, genies wander, blade in hand, waiting for nothing more than a prevailing torpor which might throw us off course. But our forces are invincible! Our forces watch over us and exterminate the evil genies and foreigners who would eagerly sink our vessel! Our monarch is powerful. A religious revolutionary. He will not desist from battling against oligarchs and ineffectuals of every sort, from opposing the antirevolutionaries, who do not believe in the exclusive word of God and prophet.

Laughter.

MOVEMENT VII

Same room as the first movement.
The King, the Imam, and the General-Minister-of-the-Interior.
Nothing is missing from the décor except for the statue of the star of the music hall.
It has been replaced by a bust of a man carved out of marble.

THE KING

That went well. The speech shed light on the gravest problems of our times. Farewell youth! The prophet! The prophet!

He points a finger toward the bust.

The mere presence of such a realistic bust makes me feel I have the intellectual capacity of a computer. From this day forth, I shall pray five times a day and rise at night to contemplate the times. In every heavenly star there resides a morsel of this harsh period.

A beat.

But tell me, you two, have you thought of dissolving the harem?

THE GENERAL-MINISTER-OF-THE-INTERIOR

No, not as of yet.

THE KING

What are you waiting for?

THE GENERAL-MINISTER-OF-THE-INTERIOR
The opposition—and above all the Bourgeois—are bound to create an uproar in the press if we were to kick out all the women who have remained faithful to you, Your Majesty.

THE KING, *amicably*
Why don't you address me by more familiar terms? Speak freely to me, I'm but a man.

THE GENERAL-MINISTER-OF-THE-INTERIOR
I will, going forward.

THE KING
I'm not the sort of king you'd typically see on the stage! I've nothing in common with the heroes of antiquity! And you, you are like the people, a single entity, you know? Same here. When I address the people, I address them as one single entity, not a mass of individuals. The people and my subjects are one. It's a matter of moral standing, at no cost to me. My mood depends upon it.

THE IMAM
Sire, my mind always wanders when you speak from the heart. Right now, for example, I find myself dwelling on this marble figure.

He points at the bust.

I believe any visual representation of the prophet is forbidden. Did he himself not oversee the destruction of the statues in Mecca? The Qur'an says…

THE KING, *cutting off the Imam*
But what was the Qur'an saying? Have you *really* read it? No. You haven't read it carefully enough; you don't even know what it's all about. Someone taught the Qur'an *to* you—to a point, that's all. You've not worked it out yourself. You've nothing but disregard for the Arab language. You've gargled various theological phrases

since you were a child, but you've never attempted to fathom their meaning. You've been conditioned to swallow the scripts and then cough them up before they've even been digested. In the end, you're little more than one swollen belly ready to void its bowels the moment the slightest pressure is applied. So keep your ideas to yourself; I'm not superstitious. The Christians dreamt up the very crown of Christ; they painted and sculpted it to their liking. The one thing their Christ lacks is speech, and a little life.

A beat.

Muslims have no artist worthy of the name. They are failures.

A beat.

We will try to make up for that lost time.

THE IMAM

Your Majesty, I know perfectly well that there are some artists among us. There aren't many, but what they lack in numbers they make up for in talent. We have a jester, one who's an excellent dancer. We have a bona fide doctor, a philosopher who refuses to indulge in depravity, one who writes mostly about the testy insects and vagrants who scour the land to provide us nourishment. We've also got a poet, a reactionary of sorts who isn't liable to step foot in here again. But we'd be quite fortunate to host our jester, this dancer par excellence, who's never ceased to remove himself from your good graces. I think you're already acquainted with him, are you not?

THE KING, *interrupting the Imam*

Don't utter his name. How grotesque! What an absolutely putrefying sardine of grotesqueness, a three-ring circus of undeserving titles pulling the rug out from under the very essence of intelligence! That bootlicker, masquerading as some master behind the scenes! He's hardly fit to tug the pantlegs of whoremongers. A performer? No, a pain in my ass at all times—and on top of it all he keeps taking my money. He…

THE GENERAL-MINISTER-OF-THE-INTERIOR

But…

THE KING

Shut up! I'll end up in the poorhouse because of him. Of course, I'm understanding enough not to blame him for it. He sucks me dry. And he's never done us any good—let alone himself—performing those acts he comes up with. Why, he's never even read Artaud!

He clutches his fists.

He outright plagiarizes Beckett and other Westerners.

A beat.

Hey, but we're Westerners of a kind, too, aren't we? Why, we're Westerners right here on our own continent.

A beat.

We're as Western as any American, no doubt about it!

A beat.

But back to the subject at hand: this artist of ours. We have values that he doesn't know how to interpret, such enormous potential to work with.

A beat.

His last performance was a poorly-veiled imitation of Godot. What a train wreck! Zero stars, gentlemen, for this so-called work of his. The only thing he's proven to be talented at is spending my money! One of these days, I'll lock him up. We've had it up to here nurturing these incompetent buffoons, these vermin, these insects—all slipping your grasp the moment you flatter them. Sham-artists, the bunch of them!

A beat.

And you, too, Imam of mine, my special little bootlicker: you take, and you take, and you take; no, don't try to deny it, you're mine now. You deserve what you receive for your services; I ask only that you keep a sense of obliviousness to the forces presiding over you and that you pass on that very obliviousness to the people. General, dissolve the harem!

The General-Minister-of-the-Interior looks at his watch.

THE GENERAL-MINISTER-OF-THE-INTERIOR

It's after midnight. Not right now, Your Majesty. Tomorrow.

THE KING

Death to those women! I'm overflowing with the strength of man! I want to be a recluse, a modern hermit. But it's I who shall govern. I am that force which opposes all women and excess of every kind.

A beat.

I'll look after things here; get lost...

A longer beat.

I'm telling you to get out of here. I'll see you tomorrow...Perhaps.

They leave. A beat.

The King picks up his telephone, dials a number, waits.

After about a minute he speaks.

THE KING

Hello! It's me, what do you think? It's me. Come quickly.

He hangs up.

I've spoken ill of you, venerated artist of my kingdom. I ask your forgiveness. I'm fully aware that you don't think highly of royalty, being averse to what you've described as its viper-like language and unrivalled arrogance. And no doubt, you are correct—I can't hold it against you; after all, you're right. But why this infatuation with Godot? Why not focus squarely on me? Am I not a good enough theatrical subject? Go ahead, pay me no homage; I've got dignitaries for that… And accolades would ring insincere anyways. Whatever… Let's see him so much as provide my incorrect date of birth. Let's see him do his intellectual worst with me; I've grown insensible. Let's see him ruin me! Mislead me! Me and me and me and...

That said, under no circumstances are we willing to sit back and watch him spit upon the crown! Especially while I'm around… He's going to… Yes, most certainly, he will. Well then, let's see him spit upon a postage stamp, or a bank note; everywhere, in other words, he turns and finds my likeness staring back at him.

A beat.

You, artist, you shall contribute to rendering me worthy of the character I believe myself playing. I shall only be a truly tragic king of the stage once I've been bested on my own grounds. That's the destiny of a true king. I strike—and then I strike again; I kill—and then I kill again, until finally one day I'm the one on the receiving end of the strike. And, suddenly, a calm washes over me. I become master of my own ideology once more. Once more I demonstrate humility, without overdoing it. Enough talk!

A beat.

The artist enters, beard badly trimmed, dressed like a hippie.

Miserable apostle to false artists, god of plagiarism, stand before me. Take a seat, and let's discuss the art of representing others.

MOVEMENT VIII

Same room.
The King, the Artist, and the Adversary.

THE ADVERSARY

Your Majesty, you called upon me to begin negotiations... But what's he doing here?

He points at the Artist.

No matter, that's none of my business; I've been sent by that class which you plan on exterminating at the least provocation. I want to thank you, from the bottom of my heart, for having called upon me to participate in this meeting. Our primary concern here, according to you, is coming to an agreement about levying the upcoming State of Expectancy... Uh... Excuse me... The State of Emergency... Yes, about the upcoming Emergency... That you are convinced must be imposed upon the laboring masses. Permit me to be absolutely forthright. As a member of the opposition—not to your own person, mind you, but rather to the regime which you favor and above all else the atavistic malice of your soldiers—I feel an obligation to tell you exactly what such a state of affairs may induce in me. From there, we will deal with the delicate problem of the State of Emergency. Excellent! What an absolutely extraordinary event. You have at last come to your senses about your obligations to the people. No more underhanded negotiations! I am overjoyed to be here and debate the issue once again.

THE KING, *laughing hysterically*

You've got the wrong idea, Mr. Adversary. What a twister of words you are, just like the others; like all the other troublemakers out there, past and present. You don't listen; you don't even wait for someone else to speak before responding. No. This is not at all about levying the State of Emergency. What worries me is something else entirely; in fact, it concerns reinforcing the State of Emergency. We must lay out, with great precision, just what one means by the concept of representation, or representativity, if you wish. It's clear: I represent an entire people, and that people I represent is composed of subjects, loyal subjects, more or less. Are they worthy of being represented by me, yes or no? That's the question at hand: That's what we're here to negotiate.

THE ARTIST, *pointing his finger at the Adversary*
He's not equipped to handle a problem like that. All he knows how to do is complain.

THE KING
Shut up. I'm talking with a member of the opposition, a reactionary. I don't need any input from you to know that one need remain, in such decisive hour, absolutely neutral. I've had enough of my own contradictions. Keep your mouth shut and continue drawing your inspiration from what I have to say.

THE ADVERSARY
So it's a question, according to you, of determining exactly what—in your eyes—the people represent, that very people you're convinced you so loyally represent. Seeing as I'm an adversary, I stand in opposition to your whole conception of the matter at hand. And if you'll allow it, I should like to say a few words about Marx. Outside him, everything is false and obsequious. His theoretical critiques…

THE KING, *cutting off the Adversary*
Stop! You may speak of whatever you want, except for Marx. I don't want any Marx in my house!

THE ADVERSARY, *poorly containing his anger*
Then I am going to leave. Clearly any dialogue with you is impossible.

He leaves.
From backstage, the sound of a gunshot.

THE KING

Oof. Got what he deserved. Alright, enough! Representativity is my highest concern—and it's upon that which I stake my kingdom, formerly barbarous, and now acknowledged by the quasi-totality of world powers—even by the Chinese. Enough! Now let's go over the details of representativity.

MOVEMENT IX

Same room.
Officers, orderlies.
Everything is prepped for ceremony.
In the center of the stage, a table filled with refreshments and assorted pastries.
Shadowy areas here and there on the stage.
Spotlight on two characters only: the General-Minister-of-the-Interior and the Captain.

THE GENERAL-MINISTER-OF-THE-INTERIOR

He's going to be here any moment now. Let's seize this opportunity to bring up my candidacy for the presidency of the council. You're aware that's why I made my services available to Him in the first place, no doubt.

THE CAPTAIN

I'm aware. I also know that you've got designs beyond that.

A beat.

Between the two of us, you'd really love to replace Him as the head of State, wouldn't you?

THE GENERAL-MINISTER-OF-THE-INTERIOR

Possibly, but it's too early for that.

THE CAPTAIN

I've done you a huge favor… Him too. But you still haven't named me Head of National Security. Are you waiting for me to die? Or maybe one of your henchmen to shoot me… Accidentally, perhaps?

THE GENERAL-MINISTER-OF-THE-INTERIOR

There's been some strange murmurings lately. He's the one responsible. It's like He wants to strip us of all our power. Even our ranks. And He's bent on providing support to the bourgeois and the artists. It's a fantasy that leads Him to believe He has the right to toss us aside like dirty dishes.

A beat

What are we going to do?

THE CAPTAIN

I've got an idea... We could simply do away with Him.

THE GENERAL-MINISTER-OF-THE-INTERIOR

What?

THE CAPTAIN

Erh, well... Not right away. For now, we won't lift a finger. If the situation gets any worse, we'll turn the tables on Him. But let's not forget that He's got a surplus of officers up his sleeve! Those in the barracks, just waiting on the order to kill. It'd be quick. Our execution wouldn't even get a vote. Newsworthy? Nope, not one bit. We'd be disappeared without a word. We'd be on the other side. Happy are the members of the opposition who fall under our fire and whose names we bring up in conversation, not only in the foreign newspapers, but in bustling cafés. In the old days, soldiers would force-feed the people courage. Their blood was pure. Would it run? It would boil over like a sauce during the great famines. The people would lick their chops over it. These days, the blood giving us life is laced with poison. It gives off nothing but putrid odors. We've swallowed too many corpses, and now the people, and the whole world over, even our friends, are spitting in our faces. This uniform inspires fear, like some sort of pestilence. Truth be told, we're a brand-new plague.

A beat.

As a soldier, I consider myself a revolutionary, militarily-speaking—but don't you dare repeat that to anybody. I assure you I feel a solidarity with the people, even if from time to time I might shower them with a few bullets. But it's you who give those orders—you, Him, those in charge.

A beat.

I'm going to try something.

He trembles.

So anyways… Yeah, I've been reading some really terrible things: Granma, books by Guevara, Fidel Castro, and Mao, for instance. But don't tell anyone, I beg you. Yeah… You won't find that sort of thing in the palace… Speaking of, are you still living there? Excuse me, I've gone too far. Can you ever forgive your humble servant? I've provided you with invaluable services. Enough to get my head chopped off, once the opposition comes to power… Because it will… A few years from now… No, don't disclose what I've told you to anyone.

A SERVANT, *from afar*

The King!

Light over the entirety of the stage.
The General-Minister-of-the-Interior and the Captain pull themselves together.
Everyone is at attention.
The King is in the center of the stage.

THE KING

At ease!

A beat.

I'm here to demand that the military take accountability. I've received the General-Minister-of-the-Interior's confidential report.

The General bows like an automaton.

Things are going rather badly for the kingdom. The uprising of the students and the unemployed has served as a pretext for unprecedented carnage.

A longer beat.

Who made the decision to open fire on my people?

He screams.

Who?

Silence. The audience is tense.
The King paces the stage. At one point, he stops in front of a table and pours himself a scotch but he does not drink it; instead, he spits in the glass and then lobs it against one of the exit doors.
Still screaming.

Who made the decision to quell the uprising yesterday?

THE GENERAL-MINISTER-OF-THE-INTERIOR

Me—yes—that was all me, Your Majesty. But you ordered me to get the police and military involved. You told me, specifically, that if I were to disobey, we would risk—you, me, and all the other members of government—a lynching in our own backyards. You were aware, I've no doubt, that the opposition parties were waiting around until the end of the riots to overthrow us. Indeed, these parties were just waiting around in their little corners, nice and cozy.

A beat.

It was me. In order to prevent our downfall, I quelled the uprising. Your Majesty, I'm a military man, and I bow to nothing but the weapons at my disposal.

THE KING, *grimacing*

Well said. Now that's the kind of clear-headed thinking that I've been hoping for. Generalissimo, not only are you my right-hand man, but my most loyal servant. I plan to make Marshall of you, as soon as the occasion presents itself. For the time being, I'll rally together some of our best scumbags. Ready our arms! And don't forget the revolver my father designed before Independence. Nor my inheritor's tie, the true promoter and chief engineer behind the kingdom's subconscious resources. After all, it's our umpteenth year as a free country!

The General-Minister-of-the-Interior gives orders left and right.

The weapons are there in no time.

THE CAPTAIN

I rejoice, Your Majesty, in your all-seeing knowledge. You are, at one and the same time, our spiritual father and our uncontested guide. Our grandest of strategists. May God bless you!

THE KING, *to the attendees*

Perhaps it would please you to see some of these groveling rebels yourself. They truly are the lowest of lowly animals. Guards, bring the little weaklings out.

A beat.

We must fulfill the full extent of our duty. It is the law of absolute representativity! Flawless!

A beat.

Guard!

A guard bows to the King.

Go tell the commander to bring in the prisoners.

The guard leaves.
After a moment he brings out the detainees, spurring them forward with the butt of his rifle.

Excellent.

To the prisoners.

Attention!

The detainees do not look at him.

I said: Attention!

THE GENERAL-MINISTER-OF-THE-INTERIOR, *furious*
Attention!

A beat
The detainees remain still as can be.

Bastards!

He smacks them around.

Filthy pieces of shit!

THE KING
How stubborn they are!

THE GENERAL-MINISTER-OF-THE-INTERIOR
Perhaps they were manhandled too much.

THE KING
Who did that?

THE GENERAL-MINISTER-OF-THE-INTERIOR
My men

THE KING
They shouldn't have done so. They might have been handsomely rewarded if they'd brought me these scum before they'd been beaten.

A beat.
He stares at the detainees.

I could've turned your lives around, you scoundrels!

THE GENERAL-MINISTER-OF-THE-INTERIOR
Without a doubt, Your Majesty, but they would've also gotten their filth all over the palace. They don't have the intelligence it takes to accept a king who asserts his political agenda without a second thought! What do they want? To maintain a permanently insurrectionary state? No. These anarchists cannot be set free! They're better off loaded into one of our armored vehicles and taken out to the desert. We'll have them lay roads, break stones. The desert hardens a man, turns them into inveterates, into philosophers ashamed of martyrdom.

THE KING
Have they received judgment?

THE GENERAL-MINISTER-OF-THE-INTERIOR
No. We don't judge rogues like these in our courts!

THE KING
So be it. Dispatch them under protective custody.

A DETAINEE, *to the General-Minister-of-the-Interior*
You're providing assistance to the feudalists? Good luck with that.

THE GENERAL-MINISTER-OF-THE-INTERIOR, *to a guard*
Correct him—not here though.

THE KING

That's it. We need men with that kind of zest to carry on our ancestors' work.

THE GENERAL-MINISTER-OF-THE-INTERIOR

Your Majesty, you have our undying loyalty.

THE SAME DETAINEE

Slaves! You're the vilest slaves I've ever seen! Imperialists! Minions! We're gonna exterminate every last one of you after the revolution's through. We're already waging war.

THE KING, *to the same guard*

Strike him.

The guard thrashes the detainee.

That's good enough, my spirits have been lifted. What a rotten place this is! It's like I'm heading up a shitsty.

The King leaves with the General-Minister-of-the-Interior.

Black.

THE KING, *alone in the throne room*

They haven't understood the full extent of my designs. But they've yet to have the final word. What are they going to do? More and more I feel ill at ease with the military. My generals are corrupt; they're all out striking deals with foreigners. The civilians have been disarmed. Oh! The worn-out guns of yesteryear do nothing for me. Same goes for modern weaponry. The students can't get a hold of me and not a single person can do me harm. If the military manages to seize power, I'll end up just like King Farouk. That's not what I'm really worried about, though. There's no Marxists in the military; they don't understand the first thing about history; materialists they may be—in practice—but they scorn its ensuing flowers! I need out of here—yes—but where to? Switzerland? France? I've got some allies out there.

A beat.

No, I'll make my way to Uncle Sam's. Nowhere else. My head! Oh! My head! No one will be slapping a price on you. But... What's the matter with me? This noise goes on and on... Gunshots... Exploding buses... All of it makes me sick. The rioters are still distant enough. Have no fear, Absolute Master of Sands and Turbans! Let's have ourselves a laugh!

He laughs, nervously.

Yes, they're busy laying roads and breaking stones as we speak. I'm going to need many, many roads. When I leave, who knows what umpteenth number of horse it'll be on. Poor horses! You've carried me on your backs for hours on end without faltering. The people don't have the same endurance we do. Nothing but a ship in the night. One grave and insane surge, advancing forward. Neuroses of some kind!

A beat.

Never again shall I set foot in France! The opposition at large should never have come after me. No, it's the General, yes, the General. He carried out my orders with too much haste. They weren't even orders as much as tantrums; I was in a bad mood, that's it, that's all. Oof! Lightning-quick! That butcher still gets the job done. Chopped him up into tiny pieces with an Amazigh dagger! A dagger from his own collection, no less. He brought me his remains, and I didn't know what to say, they reeked. No matter how much we doused the grounds in perfume, it stuck around… No one ever brought me his head, though. No matter, I wouldn't have been able to look at it. Ahg! How awful!

He pukes into a nearby pitcher.

Ah! What's the matter with me?

He gets up, staggering about.
After a bit of searching, he finds the exit.

MOVEMENT XI

A room in a clinic.

The King is lying on a bed. At the side of the bed, a nightstand.

A practitioner.

THE KING

My ass is killing me. I don't know what's the matter with me. It isn't hemorrhoids is it? Tell me that's not it!

A beat.

It's my job that's doing me in. What a grind! I've been sitting around too much.

The practitioner rings a bell.

Another practitioner enters.

PRACTITIONER ONE

The King's sick. He's unsure what the problem is.

PRACTITIONER TWO

So examine him!

PRACTITIONER ONE

He won't allow himself to be examined. He's worried he'll squeal. Pest! Get lost! The General's going to be here any minute.

A beat.

I'll come with you. We'd better leave him alone.

THE KING

What?

PRACTITIONER ONE, *confused*

Uhh… We'll be right back, Your Majesty. You've nothing to worry about; we're going to take good care of you. The General will be here shortly.

THE KING

He's coming to finish me off, once and for all. Where's my revolver? Give me my revolver!

PRACTITIONER ONE, *motioning for his colleague to leave*

Your Majesty, I haven't the faintest idea what you're talking about.

THE KING

My gun, give me my gun!

PRACTITIONER ONE

Guns are strictly forbidden inside the clinics. Even for you, Your Majesty.

THE KING, *beside himself*

Get the fuck out of here! No, don't go. I'm sick. Bleuuhh! I'm wounded! What's going to happen to me?

PRACTITIONER ONE

Hemorrhoids, no doubt! It's nothing to… Wait, you're bleeding! That's a wound. What's going on?

Practitioner One makes a move to flee.

I'll be right back. The General… I can't let him find me here…

The General-Minister-of-the-Interior enters.

THE GENERAL-MINISTER-OF-THE-INTERIOR

Hello!

PRACTITIONER ONE

Goodbye.

He leaves in a hurry.

THE GENERAL-MINISTER-OF-THE-INTERIOR

Alright, what's the matter with you then? Has someone given you first aid or what?

A beat.
The King nibbles on his sheet.

It was that lunatic, the Captain. He's shot you. Never fear, we'll have his head for this. But we can't afford to let this news slip.

THE KING

He's mine—I'll shoot him myself. A bullet right to the back of his head. But you'll have to tie him down for me first. I don't trust a single move he makes. His reflexes are quick, too quick.

A beat.
The King has a twisted grin on his face.

You may want to consider purging the army. We could send some officers into premature retirement. Take in some younger ones; bring back all the students studying abroad from France! From here on in, military service will be compulsory. Ah! I feel so awful.

THE GENERAL-MINISTER-OF-THE-INTERIOR

We mustn't rely on former tirailleurs anymore. We need to develop a hierarchy of our own!

A beat.

I'm going to call on the doctors.

He exits.

THE KING

Ergghhuuhh!

Darkness. Silence.

EPILOGUE

The choir, upon entering the stage, will wave like specters in the wind.

And then there will be nothing but light. But it will happen very progressively. The choir will come to appear inside a violent halo, only to disappear into obscurity.

THE CHOIR

Comings and goings of blood, lightning-storms
of blood! The King's a breed of stallion
camouflaging himself in the vexing features
of a man doused in blood!
This stallion wanders its way through my blood's causticity
singing
not for you
toad lips wrapped around the bottlenecking of my blood
All you're offering me is a cemetery!
What a sweet confectionary what a bloody skeletal system
of money
of tattoos.
The vile way
blood lays it all out
I'm some sort of bed some sort of enormous vase for blood
to eviscerate like an electron! Torturous rasping
blood
I'm your toilette your shit your shitter
The dawn's one
inextinguishable godly wastrel
Its eye comes speeding toward me, suffice it to say
Its feathers burst through the slate neither snow nor flamingo

can form resin from this sieve of mine
upon which you sit tightly packed or opaque
light-heartedly or abstractly.

A VOICE IN THE CROWD

Wrong!

THE CHOIR

The King sends my tribe reeling in flames, the King assassinates
my liberators! He gags them he walls them in he
paints them over with darkness drags them into all his crimes!

A VOICE IN THE CROWD

He's turned his back on us!

THE CHOIR

Gun between my teeth, I wander the eprouvettes…

A VOICE IN THE CROWD

Or a very particular etiquette.

THE CHOIR

I scream, I destroy, I overthrow, I destroy again, I burn away
whomsoever, wheresoever, I tornado,
I strike out the otherwise inconsistent King distorting me…

A VOICE IN THE CROWD

He's a royalist!

THE CHOIR

…Undermining you other creeps without contrabass. Flame!
Fish it out again skeleton retrieved dead from the marls
the leader who'd play himself out retroactively!
Only for an outright scandal neither
approach notwithstanding
destruction. The magistrates are casting their condemnations,

such is
the masterstroke of the chair's momentarily mythical center!
Power?
No. All-out brawls we're honorably reveling in.
Here they are
averting their eyes
pitying the King's astoundingly devoid-of-color
destiny, that stranger
adjoining the written rose to the underworlds!

VOICE IN THE CROWD

And my history?

THE CHOIR

I'm a salesman, say the mandrakes,
of my roots ours combined are we not one
the melted-down scripts of crackling gold which
never accurately rendered
your scrolls!

Light.

BANDEROLE II

THE KING HAS CORRALLED SOME FOREIGN JOURNALISTS. HE CROWDS THEM TOGETHER LIKE COCKROACHES. HE HAS STRUCK FEAR INTO THEIR HEARTS. THIS IS WHY THEY ARE FORCING US TO REVEAL OURSELVES. THEY HATE US AND EXPLOIT US. WE, TOO, HATE THEM IN RETURN. IN A SINGLE BLOW WE VOW TO DESTROY THE OPPOSITION WHICH REFUSES TO CONSULT THE PEOPLE IT CLAIMS TO REPRESENT. OUR OPPONENT IS A MIXTURE OF THE BOURGEOIS CLASS AND A BUNCH OF PSEUDO-MARXISTS SQUIRMING ABOUT

LIKE A HEAP OF SCORPIONS. A MEDLEY OF SCORPIONS, TO ME, IS WORTHLESS!

THE KING, *from backstage*

They're having a ball over there in the sixteenth arrondissement. Bludgeoning me with their words. What am I supposed to do, what with the bourgeois and the military against me? Sometimes I think all I'm doing is steering some intoxicated fool.

He steps out on stage.

My word is but one link in a longer chain.
What you must come to realize is that this lesson
is a grammatical one.
Your calluses, penury, complicity, they amount to nothing!
Soon everything will be gone. Very soon.
It's my instinct that's telling me:
"Those are vermin who would gnaw down the non-existent
tree."
"Your Majesty, as it so happens."
And I would add the following to such an instinctive proverb:
"Our adversaries are fly larvae reproducing themselves in
the uplifted paradise
of my future corpse, bled out
over the Qur'an, which has wedged its way in
to divide us."

THE CHOIR

Look past the King. Everything will pass. A journalist said to me:
The King kills leaders—that's unacceptable!
He must learn that a leader is one who extracts
a soporific substance from the political sphere. But, as Freud said,
do we not live on while we are sleeping? It's through sleep
the people's consciousness takes its most evolutionary leaps!

THE KING

I'm well aware. Ah! What a bunch of little sissies you've all become!

I've had it with you.
Woman,
my diamond-covered negro,
my trauma is so strong that even my name
grips you tightly,
an easy chair nothingness an easy chair never enthroned!
I am the slave of ever-changing forgiveness,
I immerse myself in pissy dollaresqueness,
Still I stand my ground and strike back when it comes to rioting; ah
M'lady, I've not relinquished you to the white oblivion
but to the countless blowhards who finally wore me down.
Am I so non-descript a snowfall? Nonsense!
I'm still here. See,
here I am. We're sleeping-alive-asleep,
I am the liquor dredged up by the desert's very imagination, and you,
people or no people,
you are the ones who ease me down your throats, my victims,
one groggy, acquiescent
anger,
making a home inside a hovel which is to design its throne
around my head, separated into four quadrants,
a glug-glug of holed-up men,
the leprous nepidae the phlegmatic erasures without republics!
But here's the last word to the wise, the sum-total Sentence:
"There will be no democracy in a country overgrown with olive,
almond, and argan trees,
in a country of elementary scripts and heads who are coming around
only
to wreak havoc upon the djellabas,
the shashiyas, the turbans, and the calumets;
there's a whole people out there just waiting to be swept off their feet!"

FIN

Let me begin by condemning your actions. Things are, without a doubt, about to take such turns your brain couldn't even begin to imagine, a brain so poorly suited to the prerequisite conditions of pure creation. I'm not going to get bogged down in explanation, nor will I narrate the ins-and-outs of what transpired between the two of us, when, caught in the very net the two of us helped cast, in the hopes of catching some portion of this world's nauseous livelihood, you opened your eyes to the sky, to the ochre shade of a dust cloud rising from one of the more well-worn roads, and no longer found me by your side. Papa, I'm telling you outright: our separation can be traced back to the first time you brought your fist down upon me. Thus, it's useless for you to venture any further back into this blood of mine, boiling with causticity, which I've wrenched open wide for inspection, only to come away with nothing but new woes. I've entrusted myself to a merciless dream, Gonna open up those ears of yours once and for All I ever wanted was good things for you! No papa, oh no, no! Get out of here, Papa. Maybe he'd already gone and fucked himself up ages ago. Anyways, here's my story—Papa's too. Between the two of us, reader!

At some point I bore the onus of a catastrophic birth. And so was forced to carry the enormous weight of all those who accused me of having wrought hell upon this earth. But I was content with looking the other way, choosing not to lash out in any prolonged fashion, only to disappear immediately down a neighboring street or vomit all over a nearby wall, under the cold glances of whosoever may have been happening by. I could see quite well, in every splay of my vomit, that the image of the world, dreamed up by man and languishing on the inside of my aching gut, would be settled by nothing less than a gravitational pull outside my control, that it would serve as the means, the necessary means, for destroying the extent of what forever churned inside me. I had to start with self-destruction, but fear waited just around the corner for me, always, and I never took things too far; that is, I never went so overboard that I inflicted enough damage to result in my total annihilation; I reserved the bulk of it exclusively for men of business and the family—my own—the head of which was stupid enough to announce one day, in a tidy little section in my hometown's newspaper, that he was preemptively washing his hands of any and all debts I might incur somehow due to my behavior, including those my own body may give rise to, were it to disappear, somehow, some way.

The story of the Old Man begins with the French invasion. The Yellow (that's what the Imazighen of the southernmost regions called the French colonialists, on account of their bullets' color) were there, squealing, machine-gunning, pillaging, bombarding, and razing mud huts to the ground, where one might discover sharpshooters prepping rifles and munitions. The guerrillas of this area would make gunpowder out of sulphur, saltpeter, and charcoal of crushed laurel; these materials were divvied up, mixed together, and then added to water taken from the artesian spring—spring water they were forbidden to drink "because whoever drank it would go crazy and face immediate expulsion from the tribe." By the time the Old Man came to be, the colonialists were already deep inside the hornet's nest. Some of the more eager warriors, the most disreputable assassins of the region, that is, were quick to side with him in the interest of safeguarding some of the goods they had hitherto defended with all their might against the prying hands of their families and the numerous brigands passing through. To protect their titles, qsars, and lands—whether cultivable or not (as if the glebe could even belong to that vertical, illiterate earthworm known as man!)—some of the quaids throughout the plains began serving as guides for the colonialists who'd present themselves as diplomatically flexible—albeit with purely strategic purposes in mind—to Imazighen customs. The

French could be seen wrapping djellabas around themselves and spewing whole verses from the Qur'an—right in front of its most devoted followers! The colonialists had made their way into this hornet's nest in search of honey. They never even mentioned it, in the aftermath of the European War, to any public figure. They believed Morocco to be an enormous hive and that this territory, which stretched from the Mediterranean to the first dunes of the Sahara Desert, was overflowing with flowers and bees! They'd lost their minds drooling over a meatless bone. Again. They seemed to have preferred it that way, ever since the fiasco of their own revolution. However, these Frenchmen were certainly no revolutionaries, as The Left was quick to remind us! Members of the bourgeoisie, sir, they come from the bourgeois class! They scribbled their colonization into history, with enormous hiccups, without ever feeling at a loss for breath, confident that there was plenty of oxygen in Morocco to go around! I've got nothing to say to any Leftist incapable of self-critique! Sure, the Old Man and his story (the two were not identical, though one never failed to follow the other into a cloud of dust and sparks; their paths were strewn with spikes of silex and clumps of reddish earth, laid out for the express purpose of leading them to believe that the slightest misstep might send them both to their communal grave) began to creep their way across the country, until the first appearance of the banknote and the guerch, a small coin pierced through its center, which, when it placed between the eyebrow's arch and the upper cheekbone, revealed a distant city teeming with gold and the promise of adventure to come. For a while they bore dead illusions—ones that would eventually grow stale as tobacco leaves and discarded in the streets. / Little Hop-O'-My-Thumb, all grown-up and clever—what if, instead of little pebbles, he'd simply cast his illusions behind him, as points of reference that might have led him back to his point of departure, and thus to a fresh reflection on his own life up to that moment? Continuing along the same line of inquiry, would he have acquired the means to circumvent each one of his failings, or to circumvent maybe just one, maybe just one so glaring that, through its enormity, might allow him to look back on his life in relation to how far he'd come? / His story laid down in his bed, drenched him in hyena's milk, and ripped him in two so "that he would never forget that his life was a checkerboard, whose black squares were purposefully derived from game pieces"; but that story never knew how to separate itself from him. Just the opposite! It led him to make some regrettable mistakes. Not only did he leave his mother to rot in the clay and granite house she'd built with her own two hands, but what's more he promised her that as soon as he pocketed enough money to shave off his beard, slick back his hair, and trim his moustache, that this house, which no one had wanted to purchase from the last living member of the family, legally belonged to him, since he had, God knows when, poured his meager strength and earnings into its upkeep. Furthermore, he added, my uncle, who is the only one in charge, has agreed to take my side, in exchange for 500 piastres. Save for a few exceptions here and there, his story persuaded him to take hold of his own destiny; I'm embracing my destiny, he'd say; what purity! His story and his destiny copulated with one another. And very awkwardly, I might add, for they couldn't quite extract any sexuality from the antiquation, which remained, to them, the culpable means of their coupling reason. They suited one another rather well, up until the day the Fœtus-My-Firstborn slithered out of my mother's lavender vaginal canal and found its form in the town's cemetery, where it served cold stew to the rats and maggots of a neighboring tomb's clean and shiny-new occupant. These maggots formed a line in front of the entryway (a fissure) down to its ditch, the same way men do, on their way into a slophouse. They had the look of soldiers, those who'd had blood and gore and explosive eruptions of warped shrapnel shoved down their throats, of soldiers, quite like the ones in my own family, whose only reason for enlisting in Indochina's colonial army was to receive a meager paycheck, but who, nevertheless, over the span of the war, would come to slash the necks of men with yellow teeth. Gold teeth that could be brought back to one's country and sold to Jewish jewelers that would fashion bracelets and wedding rings out of them. The maggots used by fishermen to hook gudgeons and bleak are worms unlike any other; they inscribe my own story into the flesh of my hide; they determine the history of material in motion and see, better than anyone else—poet or visionary alike—into my intra-terrestrial theatres. Maggots are closer to god (with whom you insult my intelligence) than you are to me, or even you to yourselves; they're athletes; they're astronomers! Their eyes needle into the dense muscle of the soil that cradles you and then absorbs you. It's they who are your masters. How I wish the religious would shut up already with their tales about how Jesus (Aïssa, according to others) took flight, of his own free will, of how God-His-Father filled his rectum full of nuclear energy, propelling him upward from his worldly stature, careful not to scorch the stratospheric customs office! May the popes and the bankers cease to defile the roots of our liberation, as well as our entire movement, by invoking the goodness of an ancient martyr, whose only equal in this imperialist century of ours might be the likes of Che Guevara! We know that this "goodness" translates itself into our homes through the word *police*. May every stockpiled bomb explode and may the combined armies of the entire world be laid to waste. I've had it up to here with these gris-gris, these rights of passage, and these parish tithes forced from one's hand before being allowed to enter the temple of psychic equilibrium! Let's go full on materialist already! Only well-wrought materialism will take the place of our questions and fulfill our expectations. All that we need—my good patrons of worship and other wastelings—is knowledge of ourselves! As for the rest of you, the only reason you're here is to build walls between us; you separate us for the sole purpose of disfiguring our bodies and what they were made to do. You drink our blood. Get your hands off us! Go fuck yourselves! The militaries reigning over all the nations of the world—whose password to the inner circle is fuckfrenzy, harem, etc.—are at death's helm, but they're killing us with the same old antiquated images, those to which the first known civilizations ascribed no comparable catastrophic significance. They're conning us, making fools of us, fucking away at the very earth, slurping up its minerals, willing to use us as guinea pigs in whatever experiment their hearts desire. That's why we're not opposed to sending some poor magnetized sonofabitch to the Moon; that's why we'll never be able to walk away from the death these "masterminds who set the rot in motion" present us with, in the interest of "perfecting the consciousness of the Human Being." These militaries won't stop cloying for power until they've eradicated each other from the very face of the earth. They're aware enough of the class war raging around them. Let's not give them an easy out; we're so far removed from every ambition in their minds. In fact, we shouldn't even bother with a reproach. They'll end up where they started—in a disastrous state, that is. But once they've been torn down by actual guerillas, deposed by the reality of their organizational shortcomings or short-circuited by their own gene pool, we'll be the ones responsible for preventing authoritarianism from rising from the ashes. O general of mine, here's to you licking the sovereign's toes, just another groveling coward who's stuffed his state of mind with sewn-together stars! Alright. The Old Man got along splendidly with his story… But as soon as the Old Man had abandoned his parents, whom he not only feared but despised, his destiny, which his story had its ways of fulfilling, led him to an island looking westward over the ocean, just south of the shantytowns overflowing with rag-pickers, just east of the brothels and north of a country "wherefrom delicate fumes ebb, laden with the air of commerce and opprobrium"; the Old Man opened a shop in a coastal town. His wife's first husband owned it. I hadn't yet been born, so I don't consider his then-wife to be my mother; the most I can say is that she was my mother-to-be! My mother reared me on the Old Man's blood and the Old Man on the blood of my mother, but if both their blood found itself wiped out sometime in the span of the next 100,000 years, it'd only come to form my already worn-out existence; today's blood being incapable of systematically reinventing itself or taking the bankruptcies of mechanical alienation into account. The seers in the year 100,000 will not be technocrats, they will continue their takeover of the world's intuition (not the man who's disappeared before me, just as

I from you), they will unveil what's to be. By that time, I'll be among them. No longer will they string me along by numbers in perpetual redundancy or deceptive phraseology, but by their movements alone—internal gazes, gestures, unuttered words, waking dreams that phenomenologists still hesitate to call thoughts. / THEY WILL DROWN ME LIKE A FISH IN THEIR SPELLBOUND EYE, WILL CONSUME ME IN COLD BLOOD BENEATH THE PORTRAIT OF A GENERAL WHOSE BANDAGED EYE IS UNABLE TO HARBOR THE PERSPECTIVE OF THE ARABS AND THE STRAIN OF A THOUSAND-YEAR-OLD LIBRARY. THE SHELVES WILL NOT BE MADE OF WOOD BUT OF POPULAR FLESH. THE WINDOWS OF THIS ROOM WILL REFLECT ONLY THE WITHERING OF THE GENERAL WHOSE APPETITE IS WHET LIKE ALL THE OTHERS BY CRIMES RATTLING AROUND IN THE HEAD OF A POLITICAL AGGRESSOR. THEY WILL MAKE THEIR WAY INTO THE EARTHEN MAGMA LEAVING NOTHING BUT SHARDS OF MEN IN THE WAKE. FOR TOO LONG THE GENERAL HAD WANDERED THE DESERT IN WHICH HE DREAMT HE WAS DEAD AND HIS BODY HAD BEEN OBLITERATED INTO RED AND YELLOW ATOMS. HIS HEADGEAR WHICH IS NOW ONE OF THE MOST PRIZED GRIS-GRIS OF THE REGION HAS LORDED OVER HIS REMAINS, AND, FROM TIME TO TIME, LET DOWN A WREATH OF ATOMIC BUTTERFLIES, THE SYMBOL OF SPRINGTIME AND THE DESERT'S FULFILLMENT; AFTER ALL, SAYS HE, DIRECTING HIS WORDS TOWARD YOU, UNDERNEATH MY HEADGEAR, BEHIND THESE OLD DRESSINGS OF MINE DWELL THE SPIRIT OF 10,000 PROPHETS WHO HAVE BEQUEATHED ME THE ATOMIC BOMB, WHICH I WILL USE TO INCINERATE MY FELLOW ARABS FROM THE FACE OF THE EARTH. /

How to describe the coastal town, where the Old Man, somewhere around this time, had managed to settle down? While giving away neither its name, nor its geographic location, and providing just enough of a sketch so that it won't escape the attention of the international police or colonial henchmen! This town, "which spews forth the overwhelming scents of sardines and salt," hovers among the sea mist of a fishing port, behind historic walls, where cargos of the worst variety sway back and forth. Isis, having had enough of the wood and metal which had condensed her temporality into one great abyss capable of going back and forth like a sailing vessel, had braved the sea, and in so doing, had succeeded in securing a name for herself. She entered into that steeple-less, mosque-less town, trembling under the cold glances of its whores, whose curvaceous bodies gathered around a very particular section of the wall, which any tourist would note was rather conspicuous. / *As I write this inside a café, I realize I might've gone ahead and skipped over this part, but the life of this book—a critique operating under its own volition—affords me no such freedom.* / The Old Man, casting himself among the cactus paddles, spiked with thorns and other forms of discontent, discovered love in this town, where only a few centuries ago the Portuguese had driven the very first stakes of European colonialism into its soil. This was evident enough from the ruined fortresses overlooking the bay. There, the Old Man could swap some pussy for a candle. The salesmen (traveling or otherwise), the shopkeepers, and the rag-pickers—who recycled the scrap cloth collected from the rich neighborhoods' trashcans—were welcomed with open arms out in the hovels of the medinas, where they could "rustle up the best girl in the entire dump," fuck whoever they wanted, make a child, and then—to top it off—come away married. But this sort of union was rare because the Imazighen detested the city-dwellers, along with anyone who treated said city-dwellers like human beings. An Amazigh man could lie down with an Arab woman, but he'd have to do it in secrecy, behind the back of his family, a family who'd already laid out an inevitable and irrevocable way of life for him. In other words, an Amazigh man could only marry an Amazigh woman! I'm leaving the Old Man and his story hanging in suspense for now, in order to set the scene for his brother, the Firstborn. The Firstborn had left his village at a young age. He hadn't enlisted himself in the colonial army, hadn't even tried to learn French, although he'd often had to deal, along the way, with colonists and Corsican policemen who were a constant plague upon the region. He passed by like a shooting star in the night of my childhood, something that would forever remain obscure. My grandmother would speak of him as though he were some prophet who'd wafted from a sprig of thyme, something of which only the scent can be preserved. She was deft enough not to complain about me while I was around. However, physically speaking, she was as delicate as Intellect itself. Or a stilt—I wouldn't say crutch; she was no slave to this world full of murderers.

Soldiers, sailors, wreckage of Empires, pensioneers (Rimbaud)

The Firstborn scurried from town to town, crisscrossing his way through the country of Morocco, burning out his life in its anarchic slums, and turning his back on his children—until, one day, a brothel-keeper lodged a complaint against him. The father of the girl he'd impregnated had done the same, only a few months back. The police, having finally tracked down his whereabouts, found him hiding out in the seedy underground of the town slums, pants down around his ankles. They ended up breaking down the door because neither he nor his companion responded to their demands. The cops knew very well he was in there: A faint light issued from the room, through a sort of opaque glass panel that was installed above the entryway. They hauled him out into their truck, along with his companion. As they set out, one of the fatter, mustachioed cops wasted no time giving him a thorough beating, upbraiding him for having violated Islamic law. The driver, a rather reserved Corsican who did nothing but spit out the window from time to time, looked the other way. The Firstborn was used to getting arrested, interrogated, and tortured. For some time, no sense of worry could be found on his expressionless face—and from the first blow to the very last, it bore the many blows that not one nerve of his dispossessed body seemed to register with feeling. Down at the police station, he was separated from his companion, who'd been shoved inside one of the offices by a cop in civilian guise. Inside the office, there were no tables or chairs, just a single king-size bed and a washbasin, above which hung pictures of naked women lying on their backs, their legs in the air. One could make out little more than the faintest black furrows of their sex; their heads were leaned backwards in hysterical poses, barely visible behind the tangles of disheveled hair, but their remarkable waistlines stood out in sharp contrast against the rest of their bodies, and their labia, perceptibly moist at first glance, seemed engorged in such a way that made them look wide open. The cop dressed in civilian clothes shut the door and immediately ordered the girl to strip down or face the same treatment as her companion. The girl resisted. She wrapped her arms around the washbasin and threatened to scream if the cop tried to rape her. Grinning, he sat down on the edge of the bed, and took out a pack of cigarettes, along with a lighter, which he flicked up into the air and gracefully caught, then he stood up and walked in the girl's direction.

THE COP

I'm no maniac; I don't rape women… How old are you, anyway? Fifteen? Surely no more than sixteen.

The Girl did not move a muscle. Eyes riveted to the ground and hands prepared to fend off any incoming blows; she nodded her head.

Sixteen, eh? And the guy, he deflowered you?

He spit on the ground and proceeded to light up his cigarette.

Heh! What a bastard! Well that calls for a celebration. Let's party.

The Girl tried her best to escape. The Cop leapt in front of her. They fell onto the bed. The Girl opened her mouth to scream, but the cop's hand stifled it.

Unless you do what I say, I'll kill you. You wouldn't be the first, and you wouldn't be the last. No one says no to me.

He released his grip.

THE GIRL

You're all a bunch of vile murderers.

THE COP

I didn't ask for your opinion. So, are you gonna start, or am I…

Just then, someone knocked on the door.

Leave me alone!

OFF-STAGE VOICE

We're working the guy over in the cellar. You gotta hear what we're getting out of him. There's some new developments in the leafletting case.

THE COP

I said: Go away!

OFF-STAGE VOICE

As you wish, Commissioner.

THE COP

What's with these underlings constantly bothering me. I can't even breathe in this dump anymore. Am I the boss or what?

THE GIRL, *suddenly changing her attitude*

It's *you* who manages *them*? I thought—

THE COP

I'm the one with all the power.

He caressed the Girl's hair and cheeks and then proceeded to kiss her. She gave in to his desires.

So delicate! And so lovely. I've never seen anyone quite like you. I've really struck gold tonight! Just imagine—if that other skank hadn't given up your lover, the loser downstairs getting his ass handed to him as we speak, I'd never have gotten to know you. I'd never have been able to get a load of those tits. You're a bonafide fuckdoll, aren't you?

THE GIRL *smiled, though it faded quickly*

That's right.

THE COP

This room ain't so bad. Every tramp in the city's been through here. *You*, though, I've got a special surprise for *you*.

THE GIRL

You're not going to beat me, are you? I didn't do anything. I di—

THE COP

Knock it off. Fuck first, talk later… But wait, tell me, did you already sleep with that guy down there?

THE GIRL

No. One of the brothel madams brought him over to my place. She paid me and vouched for him. He seemed like an okay guy. The groceries are all his. I was just getting the food ready when the cops showed up. Then—

THE COP

Liar. All whores are liars. But who cares; it's gonna take more than that to stop me.

Outside, screams of an assaulted woman, followed by the ravings of a madman. Once again, someone knocked on the door.

OFF-STAGE VOICE

New developments, Commissioner.

THE COP

Quit interrupting me; how many times do I have to tell you!?

OFF-STAGE VOICE

About a guy 'n gal we busted down at a hotel. The girl's even hotter than the one on your bed right now. Ah! Sir, you've got to get a load of this! What a piece of ass! And she really knows what she's doing, too.

THE COP

Let me give this slut a twirl. And let's cool it a bit, eh? Or I'll have your ass!

The subordinates pushed the newcomer into the office. She resisted, clawing at the officer. At the exact moment the door swung open, the commissioner bolted from the bed like a loose spring and raced toward the woman, slapping her with all his strength. She thrashed about violently but found herself unable to escape. The Commissioner dragged her further into the room and ordered his subordinates to close and bar the door from the outside.

THE COP, *to the Woman*

I had a feeling you'd been cheating on me, you bitch. What'd you think, that I wouldn't be able get it up anymore? Some crows had pecked my dick off, hmm?

He began to beat the young whore seated on the bed, presumably in an attempt to get a rise out of her. In doing so, he managed to tear the bedsheet. He picked up some small strips of it.

Get up, Bitch! Get over to the washbasin and plug your ears up with this cloth. I'll deal with your sorry ass in a moment.

THE WOMAN

I swear, Youssef, I swear I've never cheated. Same goes this time around—I didn't do anything; I wouldn't dare. I wouldn't even think it, I know how it turns you into a crazed baboon. This is the first time I've ever been out with anyone besides your close friends. He came on to me, of course, but I didn't want to make a fool of you. And I didn't sit back and let him do it, either. All we did was take a taxi to go get something to eat over at the *Luxor*, the same place you used to take me.

THE COP

Shut up! You're nothing but a disgusting piece of ass. It's because of whores like you that fourteen or fifteen-year-old girls are spreading their legs in the first place. It's hardly been two years since we've been married, and already—there you go, milling about the brothels. The *Luxor* hotel! That's just as much a brothel as any other! I brought you there because I wanted to marry you; that was BEFORE you married me.

A beat.

Not another word out of you, bitch. I'm gonna teach you a lesson you're never going to forget, right here and now.

He turned to face the Girl.

Come get this cock, little one, we're going to give this whore a taste of her own medicine.

The Girl complied. As if to taunt the cop's wife, she proceeded to remove her clothes and lay down on the bed, legs spread.

Good fucking Lord, look at the tits on you! Now that's what I call forbidden fruit! Sweet rubies!

Addressing himself to his wife, who seemed equally in awe of the young whore.

Yours are nowhere near as supple as these, you used-up old bag. No, you had to go and sleep with all sorts of guys before you finally got around to me. Take a good look at this marvel and worship the very ground she walks.

THE WOMAN

I'm through sucking your cock, you disgusting old bastard!

She lunged toward the Commissioner, but he didn't put up a fight. She picked up an empty bottle sitting by the side of the bed and knocked him unconscious. The Commissioner fell over backwards. The Woman stomped on his unconscious body. Then she ordered the young whore to tie him up, using two pieces of sheet from the bed.

THE GIRL

Do you really think we'll get away with this?

THE WOMAN

It's high time we put this asshole through the wringer.

THE GIRL, *concerned*

But…

THE WOMAN

No buts. You on my side yet or what?

THE GIRL

I'm with you. Let's put this asshole through the wringer.

THE WOMAN *helped the young whore tie up her husband*

And after we're done, we'll go our separate ways. I've got enough money to leave this rotten city, where I guess everyone stabs everyone else in the back, eventually. You're still young. I'll help you get on your feet. All I ask is that you've got my back.

THE GIRL

Got it. I've always dreamed of leaving this city. And if I've just been drifting aimlessly since my parents kicked me out, it's only because I couldn't find a person good enough to trust.

THE WOMAN

Search the bastard and give me his wallet and pistol.

The Girl took the Commissioner's jacket off.

We're not done. We'll need to gag him.

THE GIRL

No! He's fine just like that. No, I don't want to gag him.

THE WOMAN *slapped the Girl*

Never disobey my orders. Gag him. Quickly.

THE GIRL *obeyed*

But how do you expect us to make it out of this hornet's nest?

THE WOMAN

If you tear through some of that burlap next to the washbasin, you'll find an exit on the other side. He told me about it. Whenever he comes home drunk, it slips his mind that I'm his wife and he's Commissioner. Who knows how much he told the other whores. I was always keeping him out of jail by sleeping with his superiors.

She burst into laughter.

I know all the Commissioner's dirty little secrets. Sure, I may have run around with other men behind his back here and there, but only after he told me about this little "office" of his. What are you waiting for, tear through the burlap.

THE GIRL *tore through the burlap covering an unlocked doorway which opened as she pushed against it, revealing a long, cemented corridor.*

Whoa!

THE WOMAN

That corridor will lead us straight outside. Pull yourself together. And pay no attention to me.

While the Girl got dressed, the Woman relieved herself over her husband's body.

THE GIRL

What are you doing?

THE WOMAN

Laying down my affection, a little something for him to remember me by.

Fully dressed, the Girl grabbed her clutch and followed after the Woman, who had already began making her way down the corridor. Their heels echoed against the cement. At the end of the corridor there was a sharp decline. The Woman stopped and waved the Girl to the front. They continued their descent until they reached a hall, the center of which displayed a statue of an enshrined General Lyautey on the back of a horse, a steed seemingly proud to bear such an illustrious weight. The base of the statue had been etched with all the General's good deeds, from the pacification of Morocco to the founding of its School for Notable Children, which he himself had inaugurated in the presence of His Majesty— who in his eyes, was nothing more than one of his easy-to-manipulate children, and whose protectorate could also be properly applied, with relative ease, to subjugating the people, who were only just beginning to feel the first few chills of colonialism. But that colonialism and its accompanying School for Notable Children, through which that generation was ushered, had left a trail of gunpowder and penitent Christian and Muslim men hanged from poles, and whose strung-up skin resonated down through the years, like a rallying drum for the sole purpose of whisking the people off to a war that would be neither holy nor bear any fruit—ladies and gentlemen who know anything about the so-called religious conflicts—just war, plain and simple, intent on whipping up an entire population into a formidable and hateful tide not even the sea itself is capable of, sweeping away any remaining rogue ships. The Woman and the Girl paused for a moment in front of the statue. Each one looked to the other, but neither of them said a word. They both seemed to be questioning the motives that would bring such a gorgeous metallic monument into being, but their indefinitely intertwining gazes gave way to a quasi-pathological absence of curiosity. Until finally they continued on their way, which this time led them to a staircase, the steps of which the Girl proceeded down. The staircase descended in a spiral, ending in a new corridor revealing a yellowed, wooden door. The Girl, who had gone ahead of her companion, stopped and turned around, her back against the door. A worried look crossed her face, but her companion reassured her with a motion of her hand and a forced smile. Indistinguishable sounds could be heard coming from behind the door. The Woman pressed her shoulder up against it, but it would not budge. Eventually, with the Girl's help, she somehow managed to break it in. The spectacle which appeared before their eyes was so atrocious that they found themselves frozen in their footsteps: a man, whose body had been chopped up into tiny blood-streaked pieces, lay on an "operating" table in the middle of a room in which four butcher-police were pacing back and forth. The body of the man, entirely nude, was pouring out blood. The policemen had "worked it over" so thoroughly that he was difficult to identify. His lips had been carefully snipped off and placed over the coals of an open flame at the foot of the table. Rigor mortis had twisted the man's "face." His arms were contorted in such a way that suggested one last attempt to save himself, though he had obviously been unable—since the cops, prior to their expeditious operation, had secured him to the table—to utilize what strength had been unleashed by the instinctual nature of his impending doom. Shaking off their stupor, the Woman and the Girl gained resolve enough to step foot into the room. The Woman pulled out her husband's pistol and aimed it at one of the startled cops.

THE COP

You wouldn't shoot your husband's superior, now, would you? You wouldn't shoot me.

THE WOMAN

Why not, asshole? You world-killer, you. There's no room for peace in this country.

THE COP

This police station isn't like the rest of them. No one here is concerned with politics… The only people we kill are the uncooperative few conspiring against His Majesty and the government. This stiff over here—a real hot-shot of a terrorist. He came all the way from Algeria, where Cuban agents had him trained in guerrilla warfare. But the guerrillas, as you well know, have no business here. It's a real two-birds-with-one-stone situation. We're just putting him to good use before anyone else does. We've got no room left for men prepared to just throw everything away; we've got our independence and a royal democracy now. Anyone who's unhappy with that can go to Europe, or go join up with Nasser, out in Egypt. Just why do you think they haven't declared war on Israel yet, Hmm?

THE WOMAN

You're dead.

THE COP

You kidding me? You couldn't even handle a firecracker. You're telling me that you're willing to risk it all, just to end up harming yourself in the end? Kacem, go get that gun out of her hands.

One of the cops, responding to the name Kacem, hurled himself in the Woman's direction, but before he could get close, he took a gunshot to the stomach and dropped to the foot of the operating table. The superior and his two underlings burst out into uncontrollable laughter, jumping up and down and stomping their feet.

THE COP

And here I thought he'd eventually take my place! Ah! What a dumbass. Now look at him, dead— without a promotion. What a dumbass! I was right about him. Yes, yes, I really can be quite cruel can't I; His Majesty's going to reward me for this one. Oh yes, I know it.

THE WOMAN

Let's get out of here. Tell me where the exit is.

THE COP

What a dumbass! Now that he's dead, I've got no one to fear. I'll probably end up as Head of Security. Very, very soon. What! You want to leave? No. I'm afraid you're not going anywhere. First, we're going to celebrate this unanticipated victory. Don't worry about the guy you killed, everything's fine. Let's just go ahead and say the guy on the table killed him, okay?—not you. He died gloriously, in the line of duty. Omar, take care of the little one on our lady's arm. I'll take care of our lady; she's mine. She belongs to me now. Yeah, I've always wanted to show you my true feelings. I've loved you ever since I first laid eyes on you. Ah! Ah! I've been disguising myself as an inspector, I had green glasses on, and a fake moustache. Like Lopez! I needed it to spy on your husband. Oh! Oh! You just can't trust anyone, not around cops anyways. We've got each other's backs. Oh! Oh! I love this woman; she's mine. Omar, take care of the little one. Keep me updated. And you, Mokhtar, keep an eye on the body. Understand? There's nothing we can do about it until daybreak, and it's just struck midnight. Tomorrow morning, when I come back down. Understand? Alright, let's go.

THE WOMAN

After I've gotten my kicks, I'm just going to shoot you. And anytime we fuck, I'll have this gun aimed straight at your heart. Try anything stupid, and I'll pull the trigger.

THE COP

You'll live like a queen. You'll be with me so long that you'll end up loving it. I'll take care of your husband. The little one will lodge a complaint against him; Together, we'll come up with a good enough story. He will too, behind bars.

The Cop, the Woman, the Girl, and Omar all exit the stage.

Indeed, the Old Man and his two brothers, including the Firstborn, who was never tortured, nor ever regretted having violated Islamic law, lived one place after the other in this coastal town where prostitution, although often violently repressed, constituted the only economically-feasible foundation, due to whores and whoremongers alike (both men and women) habitually paying a little extra on the side taxwise—tithes, essentially, set aside for the civil servants. The Firstborn was forced into a marriage against his will for having impregnated a young girl, who gave birth that very day to a dark-skinned baby boy that the Old Man later claimed bore no family resemblance. The Old Man and his mother had gotten together one day on their terrace, over tea, and gone over it tooth and nail. The Firstborn's story, which in no way resembled that of Aeneas', always began with a sigh and ended with a curse muttered underneath one's breath, one in which all those who'd followed its ups-and-down would witness his head lift off into the air and his body fall from grace into a blue inferno, whose flames had inscribed it *Hell*. The Old Man and his mother cashed the Firstborn's soul in and out, tirelessly, to the Good Lord. Each morning they'd go and drop off a warm cake on the mosque's cement windowsill. But the Firstborn would have no story. His son allowed him to exist and hated him. It was his fault the Old Man grew rich, categorically refused to lend him any assistance, and refused any in return. Two years after Morocco gained its independence, the Firstborn's son became a police officer. The Old Man held it against him because he considered civil servants of any kind to be parasites living off nothing but corruption and terrorism. He tried to put that story behind him, but it followed closely at his heels. No matter how depraved he became, or how willing he was to let the past be the past, he never managed to fully disentangle himself from it. Even worse, he felt obliged to tell this story to anyone who'd stop, even for a moment, and listen to him, just to try and milk them for as much money as he could. But the sharks of that town were often more ravenous than he and moreover felt obliged to call the Old Man on his bullshit, seeing as he was constantly found doing business—wherever he happened to go, whether throughout the city or in his own backyard—with swarms of spies and henchmen, who'd sworn an oath to nothing but the almighty banknote.

After several years of debauchery, drunken sprees, sexual excess, and clouds of kif (kif-o-ramas, he preferred to call them), the Old Man found himself unable to look at himself anymore in the filthy shop windows without striking himself across the face, the groin, or the stomach. Why did I burn through every last cent? Mine? No, it isn't mine, it's the money my crazy ass was able to scrounge up from all that depressing caterwauling I did Good Lord what have I come here for? I don't even know myself anymore, don't know my father or mother anymore either, much less this murder of crows who've nestled their way into my blood! Aw shit! C'mon! Are we going to sell these walls Or what! What are you talking about? We'll sell them, this time; you coming with me? No more setting up shop in a port city there's too many whores and foreigners There's no value in that Marrakesh is where we'll make it. We'll rustle up diamonds Thami El Glaoui's nothing but a slave My father sealed the deal with the king of Mali for 40 Hassanis But look where he ended up Getting around via horseless carriages Automobiles as they say Completely wrapped up in gold and money. Sparkling diamonds across its wheels, its exhaust pipe encrusted with rubies, the head of this small-time dictator, swiftly obliterated by the cruel laughter of a long-ago exiled king! There's where El Glaoui plops his ass down, the yellow prospectors find a Knz ("Treasure"). They've got it all! But they haven't got the washed-out complexion of The Blacks' collective rage! This Bambara needs but a white man's slightly yellowed head and a scepter to become king or colonialist! He's been crowned king of the Maghreb, and Mauritania, too! Thank God!!! Throughout this city of his there's palaces full of water jets of ceramics of fountains of guards who shoot down crowds of women grinding saffron and parsley nuts and almonds, etc. At the base of his qsar's wall, salesmen everywhere; chickens and cocks, all tied one-to-the-other along one long string. They're getting restless, but they'll never get up in the air, there's virgins there who'll lead you on and throw themselves at you until you're willing to pay; generals with an awe-inspiring allure, along with star-studded outfits, trimmed with tricolored stripes; the Yellow with their brass-colored strands of hair, yellow as the bullets they extract from an oily light we'll never know, oh the absolute loveliness of the Yellow, with their dogs like fat little donkeys on their heels, the day's paper in their mouths Mutts like these obey their masters' orders they're trained for it as soon as they hit the month-old mark, taught to piss on a special rag I don't see how the Yellow live in such exiguity How is it that their dogs weren't bred around here; in this city what's more there's a number of fantasias playing out where the Mokhazni auxiliary forces mount their horses in haste confound the crowd and fire their weapons into the sky as if the Good Lord hadn't already bestowed his blessing upon them; bicycles with three wheels and two seats (easily stolen); work sites the Boujadis gather around; Quick, let's get out of here! Or we'll have too much to do; we'll go by foot, while you've still got two good legs on you. Yes… I know… Your feet are killing you… So what! You've waded through worse shit than this… Our barn was on the ground floor, we slept in the upper level, next to the lightwell; my grandmother would empty out her basket of greens for the cow there… You've forgotten already, she'd come and tell us such funny stories that we could barely understand, and yet how captivated we'd be; first she'd heave the basket up against her chest, and then, taking it by the handle, she'd turn it over, into the trough; Let's pick up the pace, you've got more muscle on your bones than I do! What! You're the one who's usually cleaning *my* plate; don't make that face, what're you, a snail or something? You're not dying. I don't see any mucus! Papa's the one who's dead, I would've burned down his house myself, but he forbade me from getting my hands dirty; maybe I didn't burn the dump down, but I made the Taleb and his disciples pay for reciting their prayers during papa's burial, they flung that fiery-red ball and chain of theirs straight into the sky! papa's soul water skied down the greatest paradisaical river there was, a river of rancid honey and butter, pick up your feet, keep walking. Papa's not in hell, five times a day he'd draw water from that venomous well, its walls sculpted from scorpions and scolopendrae. Papa remarried his oldest sister and a girl whose beauty no one seemed able to describe, he took the Good Lord's hand every morning, the prophet forced him to grovel at his feet and coerced his slaves to embroider his djellabas in a language that, to him, reflected the poverty of the land; Let's get a move on we'll have ourselves a thousand and one hundred gold pieces we don't take tickets anymore much less those pierced coins we've swapped out to the street performers and merchant travelers for a raspy whistle, doing little for the ears; we left behind a city which reeked of sardines, unsold mackerel splayed across the beach, decomposing cats, the corpses of men gone sour on top the pile, the fountain, the incense of legal prosecutors and fquihs, not to mention the Spanish church, which gave off a musty stench that'd make me vomit every morning I opened up shop; death shaped this city; death brought us before the Pachas and swallowed the deep-sea fishermen somewhere off the coast, or into the port, as their wives came out to welcome them with ululations and other heartwarming gestures; Let's go, let's go, we're not that far, no need for the streetcar, no time to waste Our legs are swifter than ten thousand buzzards circling the Atlas Mountains; papa never left home, much less his comfort zone; all so that I could forever be held accountable if I hadn't listened and understood him, I poured over *Arratns*, but its contents and ethnology doesn't interest you We've lost our free will, any hope to choose, you say to me, whenever I look to the past to see if my family was of this or that tribe… Or if their gold is somewhere out in the desert… In the city we're headed to, naked women toll the end of Islam; the roads and the downtrodden houses, the palaces and brothels alike, are full of whores who need but a fistful of coins to show you the thirsting fig of Barbary between their legs, but our king has put a moratorium on promiscuity, Better hurry up and get yourself married, Vizier! You do realize, of course, that if that's what the king said, we can't even masturbate to pornographic photos anymore, let alone the image of an ass fucked by one of our elders going on and on to us about their blisters; Our elders settled into the Gharb long before we did; they bore us modern firearms, and ammunition to go along with them, which we paid for with tracts of land… During The Seiba, there was unity… Anyone might consume anyone else without incurring any risk, but once the Yellow took control of the region, crime gave way to corruption and legalized theft! Bouchaid, who oversees the mosque's finances, and sells sprigs of wormwood on the side, once mentioned to me that the commander loots the tribes of the valley, and that the fquih stays on his knees all night with the Qur'an laid out in front of him trying to prevent it, but Sidi Jbril refuses to take up arms against the Yellow and the spirits of the soil refuse to turn him into stone the One and Only Aïssa is going to slice his head clean off come Judgment Day, once the masses of Ephebes descend from the heavens and march in a reinforced cordon across the war-torn field of mankind, such that every limb your body has will speak of what he's done; your eye will swear it saw this or that, your tongue will tie itself into knots, and your hands will accuse you of having driven them to flight; your entire body will be torn in half and gush with thanklessness, and you will say: May my body be burned! But it's your soul that will feel the fire's teeth; your body will rise from the ashes with each incineration, yet no longer be under your control; our feet are beginning to ache, our shoes have no more soles left; let's stop right here… I'm so thirsty I want nothing more but to drink you, but the moment you taste the blood rushing to my head, you slip away and leave me alone to my thirst… Ever since I left the old fool's shop, I've been all turned around. What are the [illegible] people going to say when they learn I made a break for [illegible] having ratted out all those whores along the ver[illegible] commissioned to build? The old fool's got tubercul[illegible] his wife always comes running to me. Once he's finally out of the way for good, she's mine. We're already married, and the old fool knows it, too, but he won't say a word, he can hardly even speak anymore, it's forbidden, according to the Yellow's quack doctor, the one who vaccinated us two years back… Four years! Since I left town, it's been four years and three months, once I can count I'll fleece the entire world, the king'll lick my boots… No, I'm not going to exploit your naiveté, rest assured; if we stop here, maybe we'll find work and a good warm meal… We're filthy, let's dive into the pond twice a day… No, instead, we'll sneak a bath once the boss goes to bed… His wife and daughter will scrub us clean, seeing as we're his trained monkeys… We shall do anything he asks… No, don't cling to me, I'm not going to carry you anymore, otherwise you'll transform, beautifully as a treefrog, back into something I'll be able to display around my neck like an amulet… The heat? Don't worry, we shall be drinking tea, no, not beer, with a splash of fresh milk… There's even some orange trees on the premises! Was the boss a farmer? No!… He's a limewash merchant… His house is whiter than all the others… He doesn't even need a salesman, his walls alone lure in the clientele… Ever since the Yellow got here, everything's turned into one deadly whiteness! Even the pondwater… And have you not noticed that stripes are beginning to develop on our black cows? I have, the cows are going to be white in no time… I'll stop talking about cows… You're spineless, spineless… Is it that calf we sawed apart so we wouldn't have to kill its mother? Oh, it's because of that… We sawed him apart… Because he wasn't coming out head-first, but no one had to eat it… We threw it into a ravine, where the dogs, crows, and jackals fought over it… No!… Famine is dead!… No one eats those withered old carrots anymore… Every Wednesday we have meat… And there's game in the area… Vegetables? There's no shortage of those! We even let the cattle have some… The limewash merchant, what a bargain! Admit it, I've got a good sense about these things. Never one to pass up a good deal. That's why I've been dragging you through this boggy terrain, you're getting on my nerves, I'm the best chance you've got. Not just for putting this defense to the test, I'm more than your master! But don't ever mention those wild boars the Qur'an forbids to me ever again, nor those elephants that inspire fear, for it is written, the Syrian elephants wanted to wipe out the Arab tribes, but the heavens dispatched an army of eagles, which proceeded, in the blink of an eye, to rain down humongous rocks upon them, big as the houses you see down there… It's of the utmost importance you get your religion squared away if you want to make it anywhere in this world of ours, I promise you the moon you're lusting after so much, you'll have it, you'll have it all, right after I've taken this man of the cloth for all he's worth… I'll sleep just fine at night, he's an absolute traitor, he's got to own a house as big and white as that, what with all the fields full of wheat and livestock… He must've kept the Yellows' boots the cleanest you've ever seen with that tongue of his all the way to Mecca, where one day I'll be laid to rest after you've died been stripped away from my longing heart and wrapped in a shroud of riches I'll waste no time procuring for your eyes' perusal that's a promise… The martyrdom of these exploitationists can be undermined and eliminated once and for all only through an even more effective means of exploiting them somehow… We shall hunt down and execute every last one of them before the dumbfounded gazes of their wives… Nevertheless I refuse to stop bludgeoning their image's way through my bloodstream until I hear a sonic equivalence of sincere repentance such that God himself has described at length in those tomes of his I never read because the Taleb would rain down blows upon me so often I was forced to flee the mosque… One time he even confined me to a coffin he'd attached a long rope to and lowered me down into the mosque's well standing to gain nothing from the situation except the threat of impending death… That notwithstanding the Taleb was only taking orders issued from the deepest and darkest Eastern fears that the nobles were busy weighing out on a golden scale and serving up to the wandering Jews (the Arabs and Imazighen)… And dark they were, oh yeah!… Whose identity though long established still receives no recognition! The Taleb was busy licking the Yellow commander's balls and scrounging up the Primus stove he acquired from a local tradesman to gain a moment of respite from his wife's bemoaning her annual springtime migraine and black leeches that plagued her blue throat whenever the rooster hurled its morning harangue into the well-polished heavens where the fquih and all his other fellow civil servants of the afterlife's upper and lower realms spent their time searching for the prophet! I'll get a promotion if I'm the first one to find him! And the deputized fquih of God sometimes avenger sometimes vandal unleashed before the caustic women and young prostrates the sewer's odors cracked open by his sexual seismicity! The Taleb's sex flowed through the earth and thrust itself through at an angle... From one pole to the other. The Taleb would practice kissing hands and asses in turn Booooo, get up you pest bow down before me... But while the leaders of the towns, among whom I count myself, were in other cities minting coins of such a weight no jackass would dare lug them anywhere, let alone be caught with their glow in hand, the Taleb rallied the leaders' wives together and you could witness, from a distance, every evening, in the reddish-yellow fire which would climb the mosque's terrace, the place where the Taleb and chosen houri would fornicate with one another, cracking open the ungrateful eye of the sky, "all of which has nothing to do with the Good Lord..." We'll storm the gates of all those white houses, if necessary, your flous belongs to us now, quit your sniveling! Heaven Death-knell Terror! I was right to muzzle you yet there he goes, pouring out his depravity and slander all over the place the idiocy of your destiny you're trying to insult me with is getting under my skin and makes me go bye-bye. I'm nothing but a filthy man from the southernmost regions making my own luck wherever I go even up to my neck in Deutsche marks Let's clear the air! Europe, however divided it may be, is once again on the verge of swallowing the Third World! Isn't it interesting how these industrious little insects make a mockery of evolution and, consequently, the ensuing human species! Let's take the citadels by storm, demolish the harems, disembowel the méchoui gourmands, and scarlet-feverize the wee little kings who sully their undies the second someone's gunning for their throne!

Let's burn all the old law books and desks that steered us into this cataclysm to begin with! Right now the globe's in such straights that our labor no longer comprises meager tasks but one fundamental undertow with the ingenuity of a tidal wave. You've got nothing at all to worry about. I'll lay you to rest beside me, in the stream; the birds come out, strumming the strings of the ribab to relieve your distress. Oh! How much fun I'm going to have with you! Let's go! Quit milling around with that old fool… The only reason we left his shop in the first place was to get out of this ghetto of a port civilized man erected himself along with their great grandchildren along with the great grandchildren of their great grandchildren along with the great-great-grandchildren of their great-great grandchildren for whom there won't be anything left to envy but mussels and termites… Do you remember those hollowed-out beams of the grand hall where I'd wallow around like a worm in my yellow excrement? And how mama used to swipe papa's flour rations to bake bread for me every day? And how papa (poor dead papa!) would fly into a rage and blame it all on the rats? Poor idiot papa! Knock it off! I promise you whatever you want just don't say another word. You hear me and your feet are moving but wait no your feet aren't moving at all you're all around me wandering my deepest depths through my most intimate stitches were you planning on picking my pocket or what? Do that and we'll starve to death Hold on just a little longer Ah no I'm not giving up any of my hard-earned pay to mama she wouldn't even know what to do with it! The first peddler showing up would grift the hell out of her for an ounce of henna and spices she'd believe wielded something of Baraka's blessing she'd immediately go speeding off with to annihilate the demons that infested our land! As far as demons are concerned no I've never seen evidence of anything not one hair not one tooth not even a buried tooth covered with earth with snails or fossilized for that matter! All I've seen is broken dishware and shattered pottery that the superstitious villagers arrange before the ravines or underneath enormous canopies of granite far from any dwelling. The vile spirits now have a clean place to call home, the old ladies would say—but as soon as one of the evil lost spirits inhabited a human body and underwent its subtle contortions, the Taleb, true sorcerer that he is, chosen by dead souls, would ask for a fresh egg laid by the village's oldest chicken and would set to etching its shell with Qur'anic verses—Good woman, he would proclaim after a long silence, take this to the dwelling place of the unwholesome spirits and crush it into a thousand pieces over the soil, then collect a handful of soil from the exact spot the juice of the egg splattered, rub it all over your body, and you will be healed—so I have written!

The rest will be read without any knowledge that he's ever existed, having guaranteed his exceptional power, having had his fill of laughter and booze behind the spine-tingling gates that would ensure he remain within a perpetual state of revolt. Now what? If his text had borne some signature on its outside, it would have been read over rapidly without any concern that his lines, throughout, railed against one single little brat whose life had been sacrificed, before birth, to spinning webs and schemes! He went into detail about the life and the movements of his character, got a little distance from things to find some clarity and settle his heart and soul. He fanned out his character along the spokes of a bicycle wheel, then flicked it away like a burnt-out cigarette butt. Went too far (or not far enough). Was dragged back down by his grandmother. Gained a second wind, got up, but just as soon collapsed a second time into his surroundings, without a sound. Transformed the riot into cigarette paper and rolled up the times around him without taking a drag. His heart is a pistol, his head a prison. He's come back a thousand different ways before. And now? Wants to say That's enough but can't. Needs to behead the asshole who's behind it all. The shits he takes are retroactively written-off expenses! There was a time when I used to cut off his legs every ten minutes. Is he circumcised? That's catgut he's strung his lyre with. Seen too much anyway. Was fucked from the moment he laid his foot on the road. It swallowed him up. A little anxiety pays off, balls too, oh my word, oh goodness gracious.

You're the only one I feared. And every time
I was afraid?
I'd beat you into a bloody, senseless pulp. Thanks
but no thanks for this ounce of blackened blood through which every
last nausea crescendos into the eye of a needle. And here's where I
sow your threads and interconnected streaks of shit into questionable throes—
And so what if I had nothing left in me but fear? You wouldn't have
had the balls to hold your ground so long. Wrap this hell
around me, enough with your ceremonies, enough with your need
for designer slaves, caustic Ramadan—
There's just
one thing I need. Just one
unseemly little leech
lured out from an orgasmic sensation
an arousal so relentless so
unbearable that not one
milkmaid
not one single arm of your easy chair not
one night prowler not one cordon
of cops
armed with nothing but
their heads in the clouds would cry your name
Stop but wait
they wouldn't dare—even though, like
an idiot, he gets himself strung up by his bootstraps
by his own hair Then drawn and quartered between two trees two hemispheres
and four considerably hot and bothered statues

out in the cold greenery and the insanity of sunlight
during a time where the tanks and prisons
drowned out the beautiful eye of a patron saint
peering out otherwise known as
or perhaps not otherwise known often enough as
knick-knacks but commonly referred to as
fear openly available to everyone and above all to anyone willing
  to sing with their fly open
and kiss the sweaty hand of death while in a frenzy picking
  bouquets
from the springtime parading terrestrially by like an army of
  police officers
How goddamned
bloated the springtime was
equipped with a helmet yet unmustachioed
it forced every last flower
already slick with the grease of corpses to spring
from its grasp it thought to itself
I am a springtime this world has never known
yet scorned the masses
with its guns and grenades
and sauntered its way into the city
into the burnt-out shells of buses
crushed any smiling passersby
and ensured the death of everything underneath
its enormously spiked boots
and its cigarette ends and its grenades
the springtime was so lonely
that it felt the uncontrollable need
to slaughter to mislead to unknot
the invertebrate shadow from young girls
and the red-hot anger of the leash
leading students around by a dream
the only dream capable of bringing tears
to one's eye during a time of gun smoke
and shame and so the student who never erects

one barricade has rediscovered
his own self as incendiary and thus his
consciousness inside the green pupil of springtime's inner eye
which the cops would dance around inside of like a bunch of apes

And so we entered the centrality of this springtime, its nodule, which is no heart and even less a lung than it is some dense scintillation of smoke siphoned from a smoldering catastrophe of yellow and black rage bombarding its way down the streets, bringing everything to a standstill, wresting away the window blinds to reveal those who, restrained since time immemorial by the insurmountable desire to moan without procreating, had finally caught ear of their own muted voices and chose to rise up, legs trembling and voice breaking, and look springtime square in the eyes as it crawled along the cratered surface, squealed with glee, and scorched everything in its earthen path like the solar eye worshipped by the Incan people who to this very day are still on the run from a multitude of insignificant brutes.

It rooted you to the spot
it swallowed you whole blindsided you entirely that springtime sonofabitch
it chewed you up and spat you back out again molded you
sin upon sin
government upon city and still the springtime
with its vanfuls of cops with its nightsticks
with its bombs with its laughter like a Sicarian assassin's
flew to the aid of a bloodthirsty government
and shouted the order: Kill, I'll look the other way and shut my eyes,
go right ahead that's what makes me strong that's what it takes
it takes harnessing that prick of a springtime by its smoke-rings
it takes razing the times it takes delineating the actual odyssey
of multitudinous cops grinning their way through as many songs belted from the top
of their lungs with their trigger-happy fingers on the trigger as they grope
with impunity at the cleavage of young girls with nowhere left to go

You look your silence in the eyes and you say to yourself: All I see looking back is myself what a lowly dog of a creature I've become
just one bark away
from transforming my veritable theatre into vision—

as many
bombs as there are breasts of calcium-deficient mothers
whose wombs swell under the sheets of hospital beds
foreheads sprouted from the logic of untattooed
heavens yet cloistered away and impeding both sides of
this rotisserie of portals I've wrought from myelin roasting over the caustic celebrations
in light of the overthrown kings fallen under the yoke of students
for whom the elliptical hour is no longer a circle
is no longer a bomb is no longer an earth
and is no longer singing because it's outfitted with astral bodies
traversing one's blood and in so doing leaving the earth behind
the earth of ancestors and superstition
the savage earth
wherefrom the refused face of man as we speak is leaking
through the student body

Anyone willing to take it apart would see it clearly: There's nothing left to do but surrender to one's own self. One's flesh, defined by the outline of a silence that's been incensed far too long, drowned under the duress of a rotten morality, has now transformed into terror; No longer shall it lean its head, under its own volition, into the bared teeth of your wealth!

A COP OPENS HIS MOUTH

We're not all that invested in tearing him limb from limb anymore. We're not inexperienced when it comes to espionage, you know: Blood, tread marks, those are more than enough to definitively identify this individual. His gobs of phlegm reminiscent of a street urchin's. If he hadn't been tottering around the way he was, gone and swung his dick round and round in the clammy, open air, he might've passed for one of our own; and who knows, he may have even been our friend. And he's out there tottering around still, inseparable from a sky of black mud and burnt-out stars. His airs erode under the pistol whips of the daylight, and we're never far off his tracks, when all is said and done, down in the glue of likely stories and flip-flopped accounts of what may or may not have happened. Bread, sugar, and silkworms—this is what our children should be begging for, like malnourished dogs their bone, or the dispossessed the female sex. Like any old shithead: another head apart from their own, a steel badge, yes, that's right—one that'd shine up according to their rank in the shitsty! Well, let's just leave his description at that.

Run and hide, me? Never! I think nothing of this sleepy putrefaction; and yet, I've been paving my passageways with skeletons, full-speed ahead, spinning my sleepy dreams in the branches of the newly discovered tree, and underneath my eyebrow's raised arch, choreographing the greatest trial there ever was, its quintessence of horse-flies notwithstanding, followed by the backwards asses of history who ease on in, feel around inside, and fine-tune an incantatory machine-gun fire out of my people's empty guts, my unsprung iron traps, and my gravest anxieties. After having vomited—yes—me—I vomit up your fucked-from-the-get-go glory into a ditch the night hasn't yet nestled its way into; thusly I dip my toes into the shit and try to dream up a flower that's extraneous to the sun-sizzled worms inside my eyes crying their way into sight over and over again every time you beat your obedient bourgeois sons and daughters who've burrowed into and torn themselves apart from the inside out to free themselves of you and everything and anything your bloodline brings with it: disastrous, onerous plague! With every wave of your flags, I hear myself scream No I can't be what they've made me into, what haunts me and houses me, one second longer, not since—honestly—I found out the only function your *causticitude* serves is upholding an economy of misgivings and the spine-tingling interchangeability of sensations traveling the length of this enormous and solitary springtime body. Have you experienced a springtime of your own, a sense of reemergence, of hope—no? I've wrapped those sensations up and they're ready to go; I was planning on returning them in a box marked fragile, strapped to the back of a growing resentment, as if to carve the worst part out of myself and send it your way, post-haste, or would've, if only some new, all-knowing star hadn't begun disintegrating my flesh, the dark and viscous flesh you'd pointed out previously would be our rendezvous point. I doused myself in the oil of that conceptual night and narrated the wrongdoings of you and your police through every last vein and venule; I tried to forge some other traversable path through which I might sow the rougher edges of my terror, but in the end that path fizzled out into an immutably grey dead-end which has forever wedged its way between my and your eye. Still, needless to say, the synthesis of this night amounts to absolutely nothing. Other than one odious legend perched atop those barricades known collectively as the Glorious Leopard of the military, Heroes who lay down their lives for Whomsoever-It-May-Concern, and other such insanities, exclusively yours, demonstrating how your prison-cages, your nightsticks, and your armed forces come to be, and how your demolition vehicles, wielding all your anguish and your umbilical defects, keep spinning their wheels over the miserable passerby and taxpaying citizen whose theatrical sequence is as follows:

A job
No way
But what if I want some other job
Mine
No
Why not
You paying?
Sure, I'm paying, but…
You've never asked yourself why
…
You don't even know why
…
Who are you
A revolutionary in the making. I've got so much weighing on my heart. So much that I'm wondering whether or not I should just spit it out, along with this lamb-like brain through which I've come to be and feel forever fleeced.
Farewell

Farewell (They leave. Remaining are power, his henchmen, and myself: a theatre which will take place only in the INTEGRAL BLACKNESS).

MY COUSIN

Killed, tragically, carried off inside his car by one of Morocco's southern torrents he'd tried to traverse, in spite of the springtime flooding or any advice from relatives, who were fully aware of the role water played in the existence of the human insect who, furthermore, wasn't even a biological coleoptera! An observation made with no intention whatsoever of altering or diminishing his instigatory acts (however precarious) laid out in the above text. He had lived out his life one blow at a time, had practically raised it from the dead, extracted it from others. It's going to float away, return its orb, its foretold curse, perhaps. It's he who riddled my body with truth, to the most extreme degree possible, he who said Drink, pay more attention to criticism, build up your savings, wander off and away and go where you wish, fix your gaze on nothing. And all that remains? No longer where you thought you'd left it. / But my boy this is neither a river nor a torrent this is merely one big channel out of whose center has arisen an enormous flame maybe it's just an accident seeing how ships leak fuel sometimes it's a long-established fact / And I've noticed in my dreams a black silhouette swimming across its undoubtedly blue and red and somewhat yellow surface nevertheless tinged with lung-piercing plumes of smoke although my sense of smell was totally insignificant and the shadow of a man mustered up his nerves rushing nearly to the water's surface trying alongside thirty-six indwelling recruits (the water was serving at that particular moment in time as the rallying point for the thoughts and actions of the character) to overshadow the fleet the mass intrinsic to its gravest most tranquil dangers The silhouette sang out the intonations of the flame's green song upon contact with the ancient and modern flesh and idiotically sunk into its death throes but not before it had assassinated the shadow of the man who could no longer count on the testicular uniformity of his immediately re-ascended dream.

So many deaths to neither loom back together nor oversee again
the orthography the grammaturgy the inadequate symbiosis
of words easing their way between two trains speeding towards
some new destination In short
so many motions scouring themselves one against the other and
en route to everything
over the paving stones over the retina over the testicles
over the breast over the earth over the royal republic
so many words
of bloated overworked editors pounding their ruined foreheads
so many new words outside an editor's grasp
outside the schools
outside the novel
the novel is dead long live poetry theater is dead long live
the plural atom of words written outside any annotation
whatsoever
the public is dying for those new words
the critiques are spot-on: They come into this city
without spitting out a word sporting a clean-shaven face just so
we'll say to ourselves Now that's the look we've all been looking for
but let's hold it right there
the writers have all died there aren't even any more scriveners left but
if you're still looking for writers or scriveners
journey further inward into the very heart of sleepless nights
wander through every one of its chambers you'll find some
the pistol-esque word the exquisitely-threaded loose end of the
pistol hasn't explained
what terror is let's lay into that word we've just buried in the ground
for old time's sake let's return it to its rightful place
under the weight of the earth the roots the tender loving care of
its fertilizer
and let's get our over-spoken over-sleeping and perhaps already
streaked-
with-shit language working for us again
so we can worm through
and lay waste

the dictionary. I'll sell you every one of my words ten blows to the head each. Open your eyes.

As I was saying…

You were sleeping, dreaming perhaps, yes, you were dreaming for sure;

Your eye was rolling around, looking for something, bestowing the heavens and the universe with a whole new dimension. First your eye, then your blood cells, one after the other, became the heavens and the universe; more of a star, really, such that not even the earth could find a way to enter their orbit.

No, I wasn't asleep;
it took nothing more than several vanfuls of police
several grenades and several indistinguishable badges
it took nothing more than a cop making his way under my skin
to bring my fist down upon your father and my own simultaneously
Yes
it took nothing more than two months in the factory
followed by about two weeks of voluntary absence
it took nothing more than my luring the king in with a red mirror
so I might drive out the nothingness of night and so that the dream of the bourgeois
might go rolling downhill
but I've brought a laborer worthy of this world into being
this laborer shall rip the globe apart
in such a way that the earth no longer resembles a planet
the dead who we've consigned to bones alone
shall gnaw the putrid death of the bourgeois
and capitalist alike who've beaten the black-white into submission
which in and of itself was nothing less than a laborer
indicative of such
because he loved them played along with them would bend over backwards to kiss the banknote

coldly removed from the factory strongbox
those on the divergent side of this ordeal shall continue to oppose us
But we shall continue to worship as our ancestors worshipped
God, We shall toy with our faith, our scything falsehoods, our
machine-guns, and our blueprints, but
going forward that world shall be sequestered, left to its own devices,
and we shall become travel-worn trappers of sorts; and in so doing, we shall vanquish
those who have changed their world rather than The World
and those who justify its blood to us by divesting the earth
of its cold original mineral

The "Plural Atom" of Khaïr-Eddine's Words

"Literature is a beautiful weapon,"[1] said Mohammed Khaïr-Eddine in one of his interviews. From the beginning, his work was driven by a poetic impulse that mobilized individual and collective experience to ignite a fierce energy in the body of the text. When *Moi l'aigre* came out via Éditions du Seuil in Paris in 1970, Khaïr-Eddine was only twenty-nine but already had three equally ground-breaking books to his credit: two prose works, *Agadir* (1967) and *Corps négatif* suivi de *Histoire d'un bon Dieu* (1968), and a poetry collection, *Soleil arachnide* (1969).[2] By that time, Khaïr-Eddine's revolt against the "negative bodies" of patriarchal and political power was taking on increasingly vigorous and sophisticated forms. But, among these early works, *Moi l'aigre* is remarkable for its development of the defining principle of Khaïr-Eddine's writing: a "linguistic guerilla warfare" to which he committed himself in the 1960s and 1970s, and which crystallized in an epiphanic moment: "the day came when I hit a truly golden vein: Almost orgasmically, a text erupted, different than anything I'd written up to then: a rat-a-tat-tat of bullets followed by a rise of stifled howls." It is this combination of explosive language, shrieking voices, and bodily excitement that defines Khaïr-Eddine's uniquely challenging prose. His writing is as much a sudden, unbridled outburst as it is a scream of anger and rapture that haunts the text and stays with the reader long after the last word has been read.

---

1 Abdellatif Abboubi, *Mohammed Khaïr-Eddine, le temps des refus: Entretiens 1966–1995* (L'Harmattan, 1998), p. 22.

2 *Agadir* was recently translated by Pierre Joris and Jake Syersak (Diálogos books, 2020). *Soleil arachnide* was previously translated by Conor Bracken as *Scorpionic Sun* (The Cleveland State University Poetry Center, 2019).

Khaïr-Eddine's major works bear the mark of this eruptive writing, detonating and reflecting its subversive form and content from one text to another. In another interview, Khaïr-Eddine explains that there is, from *Agadir* to *Moi l'aigre*, "a working cycle that is not only linguistic, but also political and revolutionary," concerned with denouncing the mounting repression in Morocco.[3] In the title, the term "aigre," which Jake Syersak chose to translate as "caustic," captures both the scathing energy of the text and the bitterness of a self-exiled writer witnessing from afar the authoritarian crackdown taking place in his home country. In March 1965, a few months before leaving for France, a young Khaïr-Eddine witnessed the brutal repression of student and worker protests in the streets of Casablanca. What started as demonstrations against controversial educational reform aiming to exclude over-age students from secondary education quickly turned into widespread strikes and riots, which were violently repressed by the military, resulting in the killing of hundreds. In June of the same year, King Hassan II proclaimed a "state of exception" and assumed full power in an attempt to contain civil unrest. In October, Moroccan politician and tricontinental activist Mehdi Ben Barka, one of the leading figures of the leftist opposition, was kidnapped and assassinated in Paris. All these events resonate in Khaïr-Eddine's writings from the period, including in *Moi l'aigre* where he echoes "the ongoing riots" and their violent suppression.

The nucleus of *I, Caustic* is formed by the central play, originally entitled "The State of Exception," translated into Arabic in 1973 and long censored for its bold, overt attack against the figure of the monarch. As suggested by the theatrical sections of *Agadir*, Khaïr-Eddine became interested early on in the revolutionary potential of theater and its strategic combination with other forms of writing. He certainly conceived of theatrical art as an inclusive and effective weapon that could represent the people and address political and social ills in a dialectical way, both creative

3 Abboubi, p. 41.

and impact-driven. In Khaïr-Eddine's view of theater, "the Act, the multi-faceted Movement, The Gesture and The Word" are considered as "potentially materializable action" that contributes to "opening eyes to those corpses swallowed by history, passed over in silence." The central play, organized into twelve "movements" with a prologue and an epilogue, features a king surrounded by representatives of religious (the Imam), military (the Captain, the General), and police (the Cop, the Sergeant) power. A bourgeois assembly, two unemployed men, a café waiter, an artist, and an opponent, among others, challenge the monarchical "law of absolute representativity" and speak to Khaïr-Eddine's concerns with modes of social struggle and cultural production in post-independence Morocco. While most of the play is centered around the king's speech and the riots, the choir that enters the stage in the epilogue, waving "like specters in the wind" and chanting sanguinary crimes, amplifies both the tragic nature of Moroccan social and political life in the 1960s and Khaïr-Eddine's fascination with blood as an ambivalent sign of repression and resilience.

Alongside highly symbolic characters, historical figures are also to be found more or less explicitly in the play: "Mehdi" clearly refers to Mehdi Ben Barka; "the General-Minister-of-the-Interior" is a reference to General Oufkir, a senior military officer who served as the Minister of the Interior, then of Defense, and was personally involved in the repression of the riots and most likely in the "disappearance" of Ben Barka; "El Arab" is the short version of "Cheikh El Arab," the nickname of Ahmed Agouliz, a former member of the Army of National Liberation who was accused of plotting against the regime and hunted down by Oufkir in 1964; "Berrada" is a reference to prominent journalist Hamid Berrada, the former secretary general of the influential Moroccan National Students' Union who was condemned to death in absentia for criticizing the regime and siding with Ben Barka. Between "lapdogs, hired guns, and corrupted holy men," Khaïr-Eddine's play not only faithfully renders the social crisis and political turmoil of the 1960s but also prefigures the later military coup attempts of 1971 and 1972 and the subsequent increasingly brutal repression. To give one example from the play, at some point, the king admits to feeling "ill at ease with the military" and orders that the rebels be "loaded into [...] armored vehicles and taken out to the desert," an almost premonitory hint at the infamous secret prison of Tazmamart in south-eastern Morocco, where military personnel implicated in the coup attempts would be held in inhumane conditions for eighteen years.[4]

Khaïr-Eddine's theater, like his prose, is rife with vivid imagery, sarcastic language, and hysterical outbursts. An ardent admirer of Antonin Artaud, Khaïr-Eddine intersperses his plays with provocative banderoles, crowd voices, blunt insults, terrifying screams, sudden gunshots, and scenes of beating and humiliation. In the second theatrical sequence, particularly disturbing and obscene, an abusive cop becomes the object of his wife's and a young prostitute's revenge. Moving between the walled-off royal palace and spaces such as the café, the mausoleum, and the police station, the text simultaneously forces the regime to open itself to public criticism and the people to acknowledge their complexes and weaknesses. This mirror game is also grounded in history as Khaïr-Eddine refers to Lyautey, the French Resident-General whose authoritarian policies and paternalist modes of governance deeply shaped colonial Morocco, and El Glaoui, the Pasha of Marrakesh who collaborated with the French during the Protectorate. Khaïr-Eddine's text soon becomes a flamboyant procession of auxiliary police forces ("chabakounis"), veterans of the Indochina War, and American soldiers present in the country, not to mention the Moroccan Goumiers and the Senegalese Tirailleurs who fought with the Free French Forces during the Second World War. Khaïr-Eddine's acute attention to historical developments and resonances is also exemplified by his oblique yet noteworthy reference to the French Revolution (1789 becomes 1989!), which seems to give the final blow to the "blood-soaked

4 See Ahmed Marzouki, *Tazmamart, Cellule 10* (Paris-Méditerranée & Tarik Editions, 2000) and Aziz Binebine, *Tazmamart: 18 years in Morocco's Secret Prison*, translated by Lulu Norman (Haus Publishing, 2021).

parody" of power. For throughout the text, pompous speeches and cynical or manipulative accusations are constantly met with a sense of sharp and acerbic humor that dismantles social and political contradictions. "I assure you I feel a solidarity with the people," says the Captain, "even if from time to time I might shower them with a few bullets."

Khaïr-Eddine's hybrid novel digs into the unfinished business of independence and the precarious situation of a Moroccan population "bloated with talent" but still unable to envision the future. In Khaïr-Eddine's Morocco, a "rotten place" plagued by autocracy and disarray, school instructors teach "pitiful myths," police officers turn into atrocious butchers, and religious leaders "swallow the scripts and then cough them up before they've even been digested." As if speaking for his fellow citizens, the narrator explains that he "was taught fear—transfixed by it," an "unmoving, grotesque, and cruel" fear that echoes through and shakes his body. The whole project that underpins *I, Caustic* is then to grasp, make sense of, and purge this fear, to seek "a new skeleton" for both individual and collective bodies. Unsurprisingly then, the text overflows with bodies that are manhandled, assaulted, and even mutilated or chopped up. Khaïr-Eddine's linguistic and poetic violence is but a response to and reflection of the actual violence inflicted upon political dissidents during the so-called "Years of Lead" as post-independence hopes quickly faded and turned into disillusionment and bitterness.

Khaïr-Eddine's radical and all-encompassing revolt serves as a rejection of this whole inherited world of violence and humiliation, which he dates back to the colonial period when the French "were squealing, machine-gunning, pillaging, bombarding, and razing mud huts to the ground," taking the country for "an enormous hive," a territory "overflowing with flowers and bees." Like the rest of his work, *I, Caustic* is replete with autobiographical details. Here again, Khaïr-Eddine talks about his "enraged and rage-worthy upbringing, at times quite calm, soothing, superb, but still, overall, somewhat abnormal," deeply marked by his father's repudiation of his mother. He also reconstructs the trajectories of "the Old Man," most likely his father, who left his southern village near Tafraout to open a shop in Casablanca, where Khaïr-Eddine later joined him at the age of eleven, and "the Firstborn," presumably one of his uncles, an obscure wanderer who "scurried from town to town" and "was used to getting arrested, interrogated, and tortured." Without naming it, Khaïr-Eddine shifts focus to El Jadida, a former fortified Portuguese colony south of Casablanca, previously known as Mazagan, which he describes as a coastal city that "spews forth the overwhelming scents of sardines and salt" and flounders in corruption and prostitution. There are also traces of his experience in self-imposed exile. Upon his arrival in France in 1965, Khaïr-Eddine worked for some time in a factory and lived in extremely precarious conditions in Parisian suburbs. In the text, he makes a striking reference to "O.S.2" and "P.3," two categories of semi-skilled and skilled workers, particularly common among North African immigrants with whom he briefly rubbed shoulders and experienced hardship. When the King proclaims, "I made my own way, in voluntarily exile, where I grew more and more solitary," one can hear Khaïr-Eddine's voice reflecting on his exilic condition.

Carrying the burden of this multifaceted violence, Khaïr-Eddine describes his personal malaise: "I was torn between lives. I loathed my origin, my parents, the world [...] I had come to reject my relatives, my friends." The only person with whom he seems to get along is Katatoès, a detached alcoholic companion who reads crime fiction and *The New Testament*, and who believes that "one might change the course of history from within literature." Katatoès, who appears in some of Khaïr-Eddine's other works, serves as the narrator's counterpart, allowing him to develop his understanding of writing as a political act that links individual experience to larger social and historical factors. While Katatoès believes that the writer is "meant to forge a new world with his every act, but that he, himself, had no role to play in the political theater that was," the narrator—and by extension Khaïr-Eddine—positions his writing in relation to politics and seems to consider everything, including biblical history, as "a sequence of politically motivated acts."

Yet *I, Caustic* is not only about politics. Deeply committed to his Amazigh (or Berber) roots, which he explores more extensively in his later works, Khaïr-Eddine elegantly writes about the Imazighen, celebrating their "unique insight into all sorts of ways of life," their sense of freedom and dissent, and their unwavering attachment to land, community, and customs. The novel goes on to offer a broader picture of Moroccan society and culture, making references, for instance, to the *mellahs*, or Jewish quarters, where jewelers "would fashion bracelets and wedding rings" with gold teeth retrieved by Moroccan conscripts from soldiers slain on the Indochina battlefield, or to the recurring figure of the "Taleb," or the Muslim religious scholar, denounced here as brutal and licentious. Khaïr-Eddine's rant against religion may seem excessive and unwarranted to the unfamiliar reader, but it primarily reflects his personal experience at the Qur'anic school where he learned verses of the Qur'an by heart yet was exposed to traumatizing acts of violence, like when the Taleb confined him to a coffin and lowered him down into the mosque's well. Between individual trauma and collective disillusionment, Khaïr-Eddine's writing is a hurricane (the nickname of his old typewriter!) that blows down all forms of order, hierarchy, and control. At times blasphemous and unbridled, at other times poignant and poetic, his tempestuous writing makes its way "through the dark," listening "only to the jerky rhythm of things," and obsessed with nothing but "the organic function of words."

Reading Khaïr-Eddine today is an opportunity to encounter a turbulent poet who has always been in conversation with other literary spheres in the Global South, especially from Africa and the Caribbean. A co-founder of the influential Moroccan journal *Souffles*,[5] he played a major role in the reinvention of French

---

5 See Olivia C. Harrison and Teresa Villa-Ignacio (ed.), *Souffles-Anfas: A Critical Anthology from the Moroccan Journal of Culture and Politics* (Stanford University Press, 2016).

language aesthetics and cultural decolonization. It is perhaps no coincidence that the title of the novel now recalls Aimé Césaire's poetry collection *moi, laminaire...* published twelve years later, as Khaïr-Eddine's text makes explicit references to the Black struggle, Césaire, and Malcolm X, alongside his poetic influences Rimbaud and Mallarmé. It is also evident that the neologism "aigritude," which appears toward the end of the book, serves as a melodic homage to the Négritude movement. In fact, Khaïr-Eddine dedicated a poem to Césaire in his first poetry collection, befriended Léon-Gontran Damas in Paris, contributed to the leading pan-African journal *Présence Africaine*, and later sojourned in Senegal at the invitation of then poet-president Léopold Sédar Senghor.

Khaïr-Eddine's unique voice, suffused with this network of literary and political affinities, resonates throughout Jake Syersak's spirited and elegant translation. A poet himself, Syersak, who co-translated *Agadir*, is not only familiar with Khaïr-Eddine's intricate and dense prose but also attuned to the challenges of experimental and poetic writing. Having had the chance to look at several drafts of the translation, I came to understand some of his audacious choices and to savor his imaginative and fluid rendering of Khaïr-Eddine's unruly prose. The third of Khaïr-Eddine's works to be translated into English, *Moi l'aigre* is an unparalleled yet fleeting scream in the night of authoritarianism and censorship. In 1979, Khaïr-Eddine's return to Morocco was apparently conditioned upon his commitment not to engage in political activities against the King, who would even later cover the expenses of his medical treatment. Some of Khaïr-Eddine's conciliatory, if not laudatory, pieces about the Moroccan regime may leave the reader perplexed, but this sudden change is better understood in light of both his unpredictable character and his pressing desire for homecoming to reinvigorate his writing. From a literary perspective, this conversion is also confirmed by his more appeased novels *Légende et vie d'Agoun'chich* (1984) and the posthumous *Il était une fois un vieux couple heureux* (2002). If much water has flowed under the political bridge, Khaïr-Eddine's importance is now fully recognized by critics and scholars. With its undulating body, *I, Caustic* reproduces the two-pronged movement that testifies to the continuing relevance of Khaïr-Eddine's writing: destruction and reconstruction, annihilation and regeneration, death and revival. This is best reflected in the closing poetic sequence, where Khaïr-Eddine reviews his miraculous weapons: "the novel is dead long live poetry theater is dead long live / the plural atom of words."

Khalid Lyamlahy
University of Chicago

A Note on Translation

Mohammed Khaïr-Eddine's *I, Caustic* is an earth-shattering censure of systemic power structures and absolutist authority. But more than that it is a reminder that language itself is a weapon, one that can be used, as any weapon can, for means of oppression or liberation. Perhaps what *I, Caustic* demonstrates best, however, is that the language of power—be it religious, literary, patriarchal, cultural, historical, psychological, or otherwise—can be dismantled, co-opted, and turned against power itself. Having borne witness to the massive political upheavals that swept North Africa and the European continent throughout the mid - late 1960s, Khaïr-Eddine must have been particularly sensitive to the malleable nature of language and its many weaponized forms—from the revolutionary phrases used to fan the flames of discontent to the rhetorical razzle-dazzle adopted by various regimes in their attempts to extinguish them. He must have also felt, as a rising figure in the literary arts, a certain socio-political responsibility to demonstrate how experimental letters might contribute to the seemingly imminent revolution.

Though we have not seen a May '68-style uprising in America in our lifetimes, tensions have nevertheless been building. Numerous grassroots movements have proliferated since the turn of the new millennium and left lasting impressions in their wake: the Seattle WTO demonstrations, Occupy Wall Street, the advancement of LGBTQIA+ rights leading up to the Marriage Equality Movement, Black Lives Matter, the Climate Strikes, and #MeToo, to name a few. Even now, the country seems to be experiencing an unprecedented labor movement revival, with unionization wins sweeping some of the largest U.S. workplaces. The rise of MAGA-branded fascism and its many hydra heads has, of course, thrown a wrench into the proverbial works. Once again, we are made aware of how much linguistic manipulation plays a role in consolidating power. Khaïr-Eddine's *I, Caustic* is a welcome reminder that we have the means at our disposal to take back that language. I cannot help but believe—but hope—that some choral subversion and hence collective backlash against authoritarianism is on the horizon.

I cite these historical contexts to shed some light on why I chose now of all times to bring this book into English. When it comes to translation, I side with Anthony Pym in believing that the decision to translate should be a deliberate one from the beginning, that the translator should have a sound motivation for bringing their translation into being and be well-attuned to its potential force in the world:

> Translators are responsible for their product as soon as they accept to produce it. The key question is not *how* to translate but whether you should translate, here, at this very time, from this very text, for this or that person, with or without sufficient umbrellas. If you can say *why* you should translate (rather than do something else), the strategies and methods should follow from there.[1]

Particularly insightful is Pym's observation that a translator's motivations for taking on a project should necessarily shape the outcome of their translation. I have grown fond, in recent years, of condensing that point of view into the following truism: If you know *why* you are translating something, you will know *how* to translate something. Once you are conscious of the potential force of your translation in the world, it follows that you will, consciously or unconsciously, perform your act of translation accordingly.

1 Anthony Pym. *On Translator Ethics: Principles for Mediation Between Cultures.* Translated by Heike Walker. (Philadelphia John Benjamins Publishing Co., 2012), p. 166.